GAA
QUIZ BOOK 2

Another 2,000 Gaelic Football and Hurling Questions

Collins

Published in 2008 by HarperCollins Publishers

HarperCollins Publishers
77-85 Fulham Palace Road
London
W6 8JB

www.collins.co.uk

Reprint 10 9 8 7 6 5 4 3 2 1

ISBN: 978-0-00-728372-9

A catalogue record for this book is available from the British Library.

Collins uses papers that are natural, renewable and recyclable products made from wood grown in sustainable forests. The manufacturing processes conform to the environmental regulations of the country of origin.

Typeset by seagulls.net

Printed and bound in Great Britain by Clays Ltd, St Ives plc

Mixed Sources
Product group from well-managed forests and other controlled sources
www.fsc.org Cert no. TT-COC-2139
© 1996 Forest Stewardship Council

FSC is a non-profit organisation established to promote the responsible management of the world's forests. Products carrying the FSC label are independently certified to assure consumers that they come from forests that are managed to meet the social, economic and ecological needs of present and future generations.

Find out more about HarperCollins and the environment at www.harpercollins.co.uk/green

THE QUIZZES

GENERAL KNOWLEDGE

1 How many All-Ireland club football titles have Crossmaglen Rangers won?

2 Who captained Kilkenny to the 2007 All-Ireland hurling title?

3 Who was appointed GAA Ard Stiúrthóir after Liam Mulvihill stepped down in 2007?

4 Who did Tyrone defeat in the 2007 Ulster football final?

5 Name the Limerick hurling manager who guided the county to the 2007 All-Ireland final?

6 Name the former GAA President who was appointed as Executive Chairman of the Irish Institute of Sport on the establishment of the Institute in 2006?

7 Which county won the 2008 All-Ireland U-21 football title?

8 Name the Waterford forward who scored eight goals in the 2007 hurling championship?

9 Name the two Leinster clubs which are top of the All-Ireland club hurling roll of honour with four All-Irelands each?

10 Who managed the Irish International Rules team during the infamous series in 2006?

ANSWERS PAGE 221

11 True or False? Peter Canavan announced his retirement from inter-county football after Tyrone's 2005 All-Ireland final success.

12 The former great Tom Cheasty, who passed away in 2007, hurled with which Munster county?

13 Which two teams contested the first hurling game (outside of club level) under lights in Croke Park in October 2007?

14 Tyrone's Mickey Harte led his own club to the 2002 Ulster club football title. Name the club?

15 Name the Monaghan forward who received a football All-Star in 2007?

16 Clare hurler Tony Griffin cycled 7000 kilometres across which country during the summer of 2007 in his fundraising venture for cancer?

17 Who was voted as GAA President-elect at GAA Congress in 2008?

18 After Croke Park was opened up to other sports, which country did Ireland play in the Six Nations rugby championship in that historic first game in February 2007?

19 Name the two Ó hAilpín brothers who play Aussie Rules football with Carlton Blues?

20 Name the player to score goals in three of the four All-Ireland senior football finals between 2004-07?

ANSWERS PAGE 221

MANAGERIAL ROLL CALL 1

21 How many Munster football titles did Jack O'Connor win as manager of Kerry?

22 How many Munster hurling titles did John Allen win as manager of Cork?

23 Name the manager who led Galway to All-Ireland U-21 hurling titles in 2005 and 2007?

24 Seamus Qualter managed which county to Christy Ring Cup titles in 2005 and 2007?

25 Alan Mulholland managed which Connacht team to All-Ireland football success in 2007?

26 Name the All-Ireland senior medal winner from 2001 who managed Tipperary to the 2007 All-Ireland minor title?

27 Name the former Mayo footballer who managed in three successive Connacht football finals between 2005-07?

28 Who co-managed Armagh to Ulster senior football titles in 1999 and 2000?

29 Sean Lane managed which team to an All-Ireland hurling final in 2007?

30 Eugene McGee managed which club to two All-Ireland football titles in the 1970s?

ANSWERS PAGE 221

31 Which two counties has Liam Kearns managed at senior level?

32 Who managed Fermanagh to the 2004 All-Ireland football semi-final?

33 Prior to 2008 other than Brian Cody, who was the last hurling manager to manage a National League and All-Ireland winning team in the same season?

34 Name the joint-managers who managed Tyrone to their first National League title in 2002?

35 The Tipperary hurling manager in 2008, Liam Sheedy, played in an All-Ireland hurling final for Tipperary in which season?

36 Name the former Meath footballer who managed the St Pat's Navan team, which his son was a member of, to the 2006 All-Ireland Colleges football final?

37 Which two counties did Dinny Cahill manage in the hurling championship this decade?

38 Who managed the Cork ladies footballers to three All-Ireland titles in a row between 2005-07?

39 Mick O'Dwyer managed Kildare to a first National League final in 33 years in his first season in charge of the county. Name the year?

40 Name the former club footballer from Mayo who led Athenry to three All-Ireland club hurling titles between 1997-2001?

ANSWERS PAGE 221

ULSTER FOOTBALL GREATS

41 In how many All-Ireland semi-finals did Kieran McGeeney play with Armagh (excluding replays)?

42 What year did Peter Canavan first play in a National League football final with Tyrone?

43 With which club did Henry Downey win an All-Ireland club medal?

44 In the 1980 Donegal county final, a 19-year-old scored ten points to secure Kilcar their first county title in 25 years. The same player was named Footballer of the Year in 1992. Name him?

45 In how many Ulster club football finals did Mickey Linden play with Mayobridge?

46 Name the Derry All-Ireland winner from 1993 who had a trial with Manchester United and who also played Aussie Rules football?

47 With which club did Tyrone's Frank McGuigan play?

48 His first book, *Coaching Gaelic Football for Champions*, was published in 1963 and led to the founding of the first national Gaelic football coaching course in Gormanston College in Meath. He also captained Down to the 1968 All-Ireland title. Name him?

ANSWERS PAGE 221

49 Name the Monaghan player who won an All-Star at corner-back in 1979 and two All-Stars as a corner-forward in 1987 and 1988?

50 He was selected on the GAA Football Team of the Millennium at right half forward and he won All-Star awards in 1971 and 1972. Name him?

51 Which college did James McCartan Junior manage to four Sigerson Cup finals in a row in this decade?

52 In which year's Ulster final did Oisin McConville surpass the target to become Ulster's top championship scorer in history?

53 In which year did Mick Higgins captain Cavan to their fifth All-Ireland title?

54 In how many All-Ireland semi-finals did Armagh's Jimmy Smyth play (not including replays)?

55 In which year did Paddy Doherty captain Down to the All-Ireland title?

56 He is the only player without an All-Ireland senior football medal to win a Texaco Footballer of the Year award. Name him?

57 Andy McCallin, Antrim's first All-Star, played with which club?

58 He played in six All-Ireland finals between 1937 and 1949 and is the only Ulsterman (prior to 2008) to lift the Sam Maguire twice. Name him?

59 Which legendary Armagh player from the 1930s and 1940s also played for Tyrone and Fermanagh?

60 Nobody has played such a major role in more Ulster All-Ireland successes. He was midfield on the Cavan team that brought Sam Maguire to Ulster for the first time and he captained them to their second title two years later. He eventually hung up his boots in 1941 but remained involved as trainer, where he was involved with the team that won All-Irelands in 1947, 1948 and 1952. Name him?

ANSWERS PAGE 221

GENERAL KNOWLEDGE

61 Name the Offaly referee who awarded a controversial late free for Waterford in the 2007 drawn All-Ireland quarter-final?

62 Name the soccer player from Cork who scored the first ever goal in Croke Park (against Wales) during an international soccer game in 2007?

63 Name the rugby player from Cork who scored the first ever Irish try in Croke Park (against France) in 2007?

64 With which club does Cork's Seán Óg O hAilpín play?

65 Name Kilkenny's two goalscorers in the 2007 All-Ireland hurling final?

66 Which team did Cork defeat in the 2007 All-Ireland football semi-final?

67 Name the Galway player who was aiming to win three All-Ireland minor hurling medals in-a-row in 2006?

68 In which year did Tyrone play in their first ever All-Ireland senior football final?

69 In 2006, Seamus Hickey played in a National Hurling League final for Limerick before lining out for which college in an All-Ireland Colleges final less than 24 hours later?

70 With which club does Kilkenny's Tommy Walsh play?

ANSWERS PAGE 221

71 Name the club that Birr defeated in the 2008 All-Ireland club hurling semi-final?

72 The four clubs that contested the 2008 All-Ireland club football semi-finals had all previously won All-Irelands. Name three of the four clubs?

73 Name the Offaly Dual player who played in Leinster senior hurling and football finals in the last five years?

74 Who was selected as 2007 Footballer of the Year?

75 Who was selected as Hurler of the Year for 2007?

76 Name the two players from the Emeralds club in Kilkenny to play in the 2006 and 2007 All-Ireland finals?

77 Name the goalkeeper who replaced the suspended Donal Óg Cusack for Cork's 2007 Munster senior hurling semi-final game against Waterford?

78 In 2002, a statue of Sam Maguire was erected in the centre of which Cork town?

79 Who was the first hurling captain (outside of a club competition) to receive a trophy in Croke Park after a game under lights?

80 When Declan O'Sullivan captained Kerry to the 2007 All-Ireland title, he became the first Kerry player to captain successive All-Ireland winning teams since which legendary Kerry figure in 1914?

ANSWERS PAGE 221

ANTRIM GENERAL KNOWLEDGE

81 Name the Down man who managed St Gall's to the 2007 Ulster club final?

82 Name the joint managers who managed the Antrim minor hurling teams that were narrowly defeated in the 2005 and 2006 All-Ireland minor hurling quarter-finals?

83 He played in the 2006 All-Ireland club football, he was man of the match in the 2007 Tommy Murphy Cup final and he also scored 4-5 in the 2006 Ulster minor hurling final. Name him?

84 Which team did Antrim draw with in the 2005 Ulster football championship?

85 Who were the last county to defeat Antrim in the Ulster senior hurling championship in 2001?

86 Prior to 2008, name the only two counties that Antrim have defeated in the Ulster football championship in the last 25 years?

87 With which club does Antrim hurler Karl McKeegan play?

88 Prior to 2008, who were the last Belfast City club to win an Antrim county hurling title?

89 Name the two Antrim managers to preside over Antrim's two football championship wins in the last 25 years?

90 Name the only Antrim hurler nominated for an All-Star in 2002?

ANSWERS PAGE 221

91 In which year did Antrim last win an Ulster senior football title – 1950, 1951 or 1952?

92 Name the St Gall's man who managed the Antrim footballers in 2005 and 2006?

93 How many games have Antrim won in the All-Ireland football qualifiers since 2001 – none, one or two?

94 Why weren't Dunloy allowed to participate in the 1998 Ulster club hurling championship, even though they were county champions?

95 Name the two GAA Presidents from Antrim?

96 Name the Antrim player, who was son of the then manager, who scored two goals against Cavan in the 2003 Ulster football championship?

97 Cushendall narrowly lost two All-Ireland club semi-finals in the last 15 years to two Clare clubs. Name those two Clare clubs?

98 Name the only Antrim hurler to play in an All-Ireland senior hurling final and in four All-Ireland club hurling finals?

99 Who were the last club to win county senior hurling and football titles in the same season?

100 How many All-Ireland senior Camogie titles have Antrim won – two, four or six?

ANSWERS PAGE 221

CONTROVERSIES

101 Name the Cork football manager who was at the centre of the Cork players strike for over 90 days during the winter and spring of 2007 and 2008?

102 Which rule was championed by 'Of One Belief' group, who were opposed to the government players' grants issued in 2007?

103 Which two counties became involved in a mass brawl during the 2008 National Football league, which resulted in record fines to their county boards and which also saw ten players suspended for the opening games of the championship?

104 Kerry footballer Paul Galvin received a suspension during the 2008 championship, primarily for knocking the notebook out of which referee's hand?

105 Name the Derry manager who briefly resigned before the 2006 Ulster football championship after a row with the county board over club fixtures?

106 Eight players were charged for incidents prior to the Cork-Clare 2007 Munster hurling quarter-final but name the only player cleared of the charges?

107 Birr won the 2007 Leinster club hurling final by a point but in the dying seconds, their opponents were not awarded a clear-cut '65 and, consequently the chance of an equaliser. Name that defeated club?

ANSWERS PAGE 222

108 Name the former Carlow midfielder who transferred to Wicklow in controversial circumstances in 2007?

109 Tyrone won the 2007 Ulster minor football title by a point but television replays subsequently showed that one of their points was actually wide. Who did Tyrone defeat in that final?

110 Name the Kildare club who had two players suspended for their 2007 Leinster club football semi-final after incidents arising from their quarter-final second replay?

111 Which year did Tipperary withdraw from the All-Ireland qualifiers over a dispute with the county board over the fixing of club hurling matches prior to their first-round clash with Fermanagh?

112 Which inter-county football squad went on strike in 2004?

113 Which inter-county hurling squad went on strike for a brief period in the summer of 2005?

114 In 2007, three Munster counties pulled their players out of participation in the Munster football Interprovincial competition in protest at the altered Munster football draw, which seeded Cork and Kerry. Apart from Cork and Kerry though, name the only other county that had representatives on that year's team?

115 Which former All-Star winner auctioned off his award in protest at his son's failure to secure an All-Star award in 2005?

ANSWERS PAGE 222

116 Name the Kilkenny hurler who was dropped for the 2000 All-Ireland final for playing a local soccer game the week beforehand?

117 Name the former Kerry player who removed his father's All-Ireland medals from display in Croke Park in protest at the England rugby team playing at the venue in 2007?

118 Who refereed the hugely controversial replayed Munster hurling final between Clare and Waterford in 1998?

119 Which college were thrown out of the 2008 Sigerson Cup at the quarter-final stage – before being reinstated – after playing an illegal player in their previous match?

120 Why did controversy surface in the immediate aftermath of the 2005 Christy Ring Cup final between Westmeath and Down?

CLUBCALL 1

Name the county of the following clubs

121 Carrigtwohill

122 Mullinavat

123 Meelick-Eyrecourt

124 Clonoulty-Rossmore

125 Carrickcruppin

126 Kenmare

127 Carbery Rangers

128 Clooney-Quin

129 Breaffy

130 Tallow

131 Ballinteer/St John's

132 An Ríocht

133 Kileeshil

134 Drumcollogher/Broadford

135 Kingscourt

136 Coolderry

137 Kilmainhamwood

138 Ballymahon

139 Ballindereen

140 Newtownbutler

ANSWERS PAGE 222

NEW, SECONDARY AND NOW DEFUNCT COMPETITIONS

141 The McGrath Cup is played in which province?

142 Which county won the Dr McKenna Cup four times in a row between 2004-07?

143 The O'Byrne Cup is played in which province?

144 In which year were the All-Ireland Junior and Intermediate club championships inaugurated (it was in the last five years)?

145 Kevin Flynn captained which county to their first Walsh Cup in 37 years in 2003?

146 The Dr Lagan Cup is a now defunct competition that was played in which province between 1943 and 1967?

147 Tommy Larkin's were defeated in the 2008 All-Ireland Intermediate hurling final. From which county do they hail?

148 Although UCD won the Walsh Cup in 2004, the 2008 final was won by a county from outside the province for the first time in history. Which county?

149 The Kehoe Cup is a hurling competition played in which province?

150 Name the only two counties to win an All-Ireland B Football title and to also play in an All-Ireland senior football semi-final (prior to 2008)?

ANSWERS PAGE 222

151 Canovee won the 2008 All-Ireland club junior football title. From which county do they hail?

152 Apart from Galway, which other two counties have won Connacht hurling titles?

153 Between 1985 and 1995, London won which All-Ireland hurling competition five times?

154 The Thomond Feis was a hurling competition played between 1913-56 (although there was no competition for ten of those years) in which province?

155 Robert Emmett's won the All-Ireland Intermediate hurling title in 2007 but which county were they representing?

156 Name the Kerry club that won the All-Ireland junior club football title in 2006 and who sensationally won the All-Ireland Intermediate club football title a year later?

157 Paul Clancy won All-Ireland senior football medals with Galway in 1998 and 2001 but he also won an All-Ireland Intermediate club football medal in 2008 with which club?

158 Name the only club to contest a Munster club football final and an All-Ireland junior club hurling final?

159 In the 1950s and 1960s, an annual hurling competition was played in which famous English stadium?

160 Name the trophy awarded for the winners of the above competition?

ANSWERS PAGE 222

ARMAGH GENERAL KNOWLEDGE

161 Prior to 2008, who were the last club to defeat Crossmaglen in the senior football championship in Armagh?

162 Who defeated Keady in the 2008 All-Ireland Intermediate hurling semi-final?

163 Who managed Armagh to the 1994 National Football league final?

164 Who did Armagh defeat in the 1994 National Football league semi-final?

165 Name the player who was sent off in the 1999 All-Ireland football semi-final against Meath?

166 Who defeated Armagh in the 2007 Nicky Rackard Cup final?

167 Who captained Armagh to the 2006 All-Ireland Ladies Football final?

168 True or False? When Armagh defeated Cavan in the 2008 Ulster football championship, it was the first time they'd ever won a championship match against Cavan in Breffni Park.

169 Who defeated Armagh in the 2007 All-Ireland U-21 football semi-final?

170 In which year did Enda McNulty and the McEntee twins win an Ulster minor football title?

171 Which Armagh club won an All-Ireland junior club Camogie title in 2003?

ANSWERS PAGE 222

172 In the 1993 Ulster championship quarter-final replay, Armagh looked dead and buried when they trailed by nine points with seven minutes remaining before storming back to win by a point. Which team did they sensationally defeat that day?

173 In the above game, name the Armagh forward who scored 2-1 in those closing minutes to help Armagh secure a famous win?

174 In which year did Armagh reach the Division One National League Camogie final for the first and only time – 1994, 1995 or 1996?

175 Name the only Ulster club to defeat Crossmaglen more than once in the Ulster club championship?

176 Name the two co-trainers who managed Armagh to the 2006 All-Ireland ladies senior football final?

177 In which year did Armagh sensationally reach the All-Ireland minor Camogie final – 1987, 1988 or 1989?

178 Name three of the five clubs that defeated Crossmaglen in the Ulster club championship between 1996 and 2006?

179 Name the Armagh player who played in the 1988 All-Ireland Junior Camogie final and in the 2006 All-Ireland ladies senior football final?

180 When Armagh lost to Down in the 1992 Ulster championship, what record (which they had held since 1969) did they lose that day?

NICKNAMES

181 Denis Moran (Kerry footballer)

182 Michael Walsh (Waterford hurler)

183 Diarmuid O'Sullivan (Cork hurler)

184 Ger O'Grady (Tipperary hurler)

185 Eugene Hughes (Monaghan footballer)

186 Michael Fagan (Westmeath footballer)

187 Owen Mulligan (Tyrone footballer)

188 Tony Regan (Roscommon footballer)

189 Seamus McEnaney (Monaghan football manager)

190 MJ Flaherty (Galway hurler and manager)

191 Ger O'Loughlin (Clare hurler)

192 Ryan McMenamin (Tyrone footballer)

193 Pat Heffernan (Limerick hurler)

194 Sean Daly (Waterford hurler)

195 Mickey Byrne (Tipperary hurler)

196 PJ O'Connell (Clare hurler)

197 Bill Gannon (Kildare footballer)

198 Paddy Collins (Cork hurler)

199 Brian Whelahan (Offaly hurler)

200 Kevin Hughes (Tyrone footballer)

ANSWERS PAGE 222

TRUE OR FALSE

201 Tom O'Sullivan captained Munster to the 2007 Interprovincial football title.

202 Nicky Rackard was selected on the GAA's Hurling Team of the Millennium.

203 Christy Ring won his eighth All-Ireland senior hurling medal in 1954.

204 Prior to 2008, Westmeath had never beaten Meath in the football championship.

205 Dublin beat Kilkenny in the 2007 Leinster U-21 hurling final.

206 When Wexford defeated Tipperary in the 2007 All-Ireland hurling quarter-final, it was their first championship win over Tipp since 1968.

207 Down have never lost to Kerry in the senior football championship.

208 Galway defeated Tyrone in the 2007 All-Ireland minor football final.

209 A Waterford club has never won an All-Ireland club hurling title.

210 A Tyrone club has never contested an All-Ireland club football final.

ANSWERS PAGE 222

211 Kerry and Cork share the same number of All-Ireland U-21 football titles.

212 Crossmaglen Rangers defeated Ballinderry in the 2007 Ulster club football final.

213 The Offaly senior hurlers haven't won a Leinster title since 1995.

214 Prior to 2008, Leinster is the only province to have produced two winners of the Tommy Murphy Cup.

215 Setanta Ó hAilpín never played senior football for Cork.

216 Limerick have never won a Munster football title.

217 UCD and Crossmaglen Rangers are the only two clubs in the country to win back-to-back All-Ireland club football titles.

218 In 2007, Cork became the first team to lose two games in the hurling championship and still reach an All-Ireland quarter-final.

219 Pat Fanning was the only GAA President from Waterford.

220 Prior to 2008, Nemo Rangers had never won four Cork county football titles in a row.

CARLOW GENERAL KNOWLEDGE

221 Name the former Waterford hurler who managed Carlow to the 2008 Division Two National Hurling League final?

222 In which year did Éire Óg lose an All-Ireland club semi-final to Crossmaglen Rangers?

223 Name the Dublin club that St Mullin's defeated in the 2002 Leinster club hurling championship?

224 Which club defeated O'Hanrahan's in the 2001 All-Ireland club semi-final?

225 Who defeated Carlow in the 2005 Division Two National League hurling final?

226 Name the former Carlow football manager, who was a senior hurling selector in 2008?

227 In what season did Carlow make their lone National Football League final appearance?

228 Name the two clubs that Éire Óg defeated in All-Ireland club football semi-finals?

229 Name the Kilkenny man who managed Carlow to the 2006 Leinster minor hurling final?

230 Name the Carlow minor football captain in 2007 who made his senior championship debut against Meath in 2008?

ANSWERS PAGE 222

231 Who did Knockbeg College defeat to win the All-Ireland Colleges football title in 2005?

232 Name the former Éire Óg Carlow and Carlow footballer who transferred to Kildare in the 1990s?

233 Name the Carlow dual star who played in the drawn 1973 Railway Cup final with the Combined Universities?

234 Who captained Carlow to the All-Ireland 'B' Senior Hurling Championship title in 1992?

235 Who captained Carlow to the All-Ireland 'B' Senior Football title in 1994?

236 Two players featured on the starting fifteen in both the 1992 All-Ireland SHC B final and the 1994 All-Ireland SFC B final triumphs. Name them?

237 Name the Carlow dual star who won a Railway Cup hurling medal as a mid-fielder in 1979 and who also played football with Leinster?

238 True or False? Carlow once beat a Cork side with Christy Ring in a National Hurling league game in Dr Cullen Park.

239 In 2004, Pat Coady became the highest scoring hurler in Carlow history, breaking a record which had stood since the 1960s. Name the player whose record Coady broke?

240 Name the only Carlow player to captain Leinster to a Railway Cup title?

ANSWERS PAGE 222

ALL-IRELAND FINAL RTÉ MAN OF THE MATCH IN THE LAST 15 YEARS

241 Name the Kilkenny forward who hit 1-5 from play in the 2007 All-Ireland hurling final?

242 Name the Kerry defender who was selected after the 2006 final?

243 Cork's Niall McCarthy was given the hurling award in which year?

244 Which Galway forward won the award in 1998 – Michael Donnellan or Padraig Joyce?

245 Prior to 2008, which year was Kilkenny's Noel Hickey selected for the award?

246 What year was Ollie Baker selected for the hurling award?

247 Name the Tyrone player selected in 2003?

248 Name the Wexford central defender selected in 1996?

249 Name the only hurler to captain his team to an All-Ireland and also pick up the man-of-the-match award (prior to 2008)?

250 Maurice Fitzgerald won the award in 1997 after scoring how many points out of Kerry's total of 0.13?

ANSWERS PAGE 223

251 Name the Down forward who was selected as man-of-the-match in almost every match the county played in the 1994 championship, including the final?

252 Name the Cork hurler who won the award in 2005?

253 Name the Cork defender who was given the award after the 1999 final?

254 Clare's Sean McMahon won the award in which year's final?

255 Prior to 2008, name the only hurler to win two man-of-the-match awards in the last 15 years?

256 Prior to 2008, name the only footballer to win two man-of-the-match awards in the last 15 years?

257 In which year's final was DJ Carey selected as man-of-the-match?

258 Which hurler won the award in 2006, even though it was only his third championship start for the county?

259 Name the Derry defender selected after the 1993 football final?

260 Prior to 2008, name the only player (hurling or football) to be selected as man of the match from the losing All-Ireland finalists?

ANSWERS PAGE 223

SENIOR CAMOGIE AND LADIES' FOOTBALL

CAMOGIE

261 Name the former Wexford Camogie player who managed the county to the 2007 All-Ireland title?

262 Which province won the Gael Linn Interprovincial Camogie title for the first time in 40 years in 2007?

263 Which college won the 2008 Ashbourne Cup?

264 In which year did the Camogie Association celebrate its Centenary year – 2002, 2003 or 2004?

265 Who captained Wexford to the 2007 All-Ireland title?

266 Name the former Cork camogie star who works as a sports journalist with the *Irish Examiner* and *Evening Echo*?

267 Which county won the National League in 2008 for the first time in 15 years?

268 True or False? Cork and Tipperary are the only Munster counties to win an All-Ireland senior Camogie title.

269 She won an All-Ireland medal with Cork in 2006 as well as an All-Star award. As a member of the Irish Defence Forces, she was presented with her All-Star award in Liberia by President Mary McAleese. Name her?

270 Name the former Tipperary hurler and All-Star who coached the county to their first All-Ireland title in 1999?

LADIES' FOOTBALL

271 Name the player who captained Cork to three All-Ireland titles in a row between 2005-07?

272 Name the former Mayo hurling manager who managed Mayo to the 2007 All-Ireland final?

273 Name the Cork inside forward who scored goals in the 2005 and 2007 All-Ireland finals?

274 Name the only county to go from winning an All-Ireland junior football title to reaching an All-Ireland senior football final within the space of 12 months (it happened in the last decade)?

275 Which county won the 2008 Ladies' National Football league title?

276 Which county halted Cork's 31-game unbeaten run by beating them in the 2007 National league semi-final?

277 Prior to 2008, name the only two Ulster counties to have won a senior ladies' football title?

278 Name the Waterford hurling selector from 2007 and 2008 who managed Waterford ladies to five All-Ireland senior football titles?

279 What is the name of the Cup presented to the All-Ireland senior ladies' football champions?

280 The daughter of a former All-Ireland winning manager (from another province) played with Armagh in the 2006 All-Ireland football final. Name either the father or the daughter?

CAVAN GENERAL KNOWLEDGE

281 Prior to 2008, name Cavan's only two All-Stars?

282 Name the first captain to bring the Sam Maguire to Ulster?

283 Prior to 2008, who were the last Cavan club to reach an Ulster club football final?

284 In which year did St Patrick's, Cavan win their only All-Ireland Colleges football title – 1972, 1973 or 1974?

285 Name the former Armagh All-Ireland medal winner who coached Mullahoran to the 2006 Cavan county senior football title?

286 In which season did Martin McHugh first take charge of Cavan?

287 Name the Cavan All-Ireland medal winner from 1947 and 1948 who died at the age of just 25 in 1949?

288 Before he transferred to Cavan Gaels, with which club did Anthony Forde play?

289 Name the goalkeeper on the Cavan team which reached the 2002 National League final?

290 When Cavan won their last All-Ireland title in 1952, their team included Des and Liam Maguire. But name their brother, who lined out against them for Meath in that All-Ireland final?

291 Prior to 2008, name the Cavan player who was the joint leading goalscorer in Ulster football championship history?

292 Which county defeated Cavan in the 1988 All-Ireland U-21 football final?

293 Name the two brothers who played on the Ulster senior title winning team of 1997?

294 In which year did Cavan first appear in an All-Ireland senior football final?

295 Who defeated Cavan in the 1967 All-Ireland football semi-final?

296 Name the only Cavan player selected in 1984 on the team of greatest players never to win an All-Ireland?

297 Name three of the four Cavan players to play International Rules?

298 How many All-Ireland minor football finals have Cavan appeared in – three, four or five?

299 Although Mullahoran, St Joseph's have been nominated as county hurling champions every year since 1990, which club holds the record number of senior hurling titles?

300 After scoring eight of Cavan's eleven points in the 1947 All-Ireland final in the Polo Grounds in New York, what nickname did some American sportswriters put on Peter Donohue?

ANSWERS PAGE 223

NAME THE YEAR

301 Sean McCague takes over as GAA President.

302 Conor Hayes manages Galway to an All-Ireland senior hurling final.

303 Offaly footballers win their first National Football league title.

304 Declan O'Sullivan captains Kerry in an All-Ireland senior football final for the first time.

305 Tyrone win the National football league title for the second time in their history and for the second year in succession.

306 Limerick Institute of Technology win the Fitzgibbon Cup for the first time.

307 Padraig Horan manages Birr to an All-Ireland club title.

308 Mickey Harte manages Tyrone to an All-Ireland U-21 title for the first time in his managerial career.

309 Ger Loughnane steps down as Clare manager.

310 Kerry and Dublin meet in a drawn and replayed All-Ireland football quarter-final in Thurles.

311 Páidí Ó Sé departs Kerry as manager.

ANSWERS PAGE 223

312 Derry win their third National Football league title in the 1990s.

313 Clare contest an All-Ireland minor hurling final for the first time (it happened in the last 25 years).

314 Kilkenny narrowly defeat Antrim in an All-Ireland hurling semi-final in Dundalk (it was played in the last 25 years).

315 In his first season as Cork manager, Limerick hammer Jimmy Barry Murphy's Cork in the Munster championship.

316 Maurice Fitzgerald plays in his last Munster senior final for Kerry.

317 Matty Murphy leads Galway to his first of four All-Ireland minor hurling titles won as manager (prior to 2008).

318 Toomevara defeat Mount Sion in a Munster club hurling final after a late scoring surge.

319 Mick O'Dwyer manages Kerry for the last time.

320 Brian Cody plays at full-forward in an All-Ireland senior hurling final for Kilkenny.

ANSWERS PAGE 223

FILL IN THE MISSING PARTS IN THE CLUB NAMES 1

321 Ballina

322 Oulart-the-

323 Laune

324 Crossmolina

325 Castlebar

326 Enniskillen

327 Ballycastle

328 Thurles

329 Moate

330 Ballinderry

331 Tuam

332 Castleblayney

333 Dunmore

334 Dunloy

335 Mullingar

336 Kilrush

337 Clonmel

338 Faythe

339 Melvin

340 Derrygonnelly

ANSWERS PAGE 223

CLARE GENERAL KNOWLEDGE

341 Name the only Clare club to win county hurling titles in three different centuries?

342 Who managed Clare to the 1997 All-Ireland minor hurling title?

343 In which year did Clare win the All-Ireland B football championship?

344 Apart from St Flannan's College, name the only other Clare school to win the Dr Harty Cup?

345 Name three of the four Clare clubs to contest Munster club football finals?

346 In which year did Clare win their only Munster senior ladies football title (it happened in the last ten years)?

347 In which year did Clare last reach a National hurling league final?

348 In which year did St Flannan's College last win an All-Ireland Colleges title?

349 Name the Soviet Airline which sponsored the Clare hurlers in 1991 and 1992?

350 In which year did Clare last contest a Division One National Football league semi-final (it happened in the last 15 years)?

ANSWERS PAGE 223

351 Who captained Clare in the 2008 Munster hurling final?

352 Which club defeated Doonbeg in the 1999 All-Ireland club football semi-final?

353 In the hugely controversial 2008 Munster U-21 hurling final, name the Clare goalkeeper who was penalised for stepping outside the square in the dying minutes, which led to the controversy?

354 Which club has won the most Clare senior football championships?

355 Name the only Clare hurler in the top 20 all-time senior hurling championship scorers?

356 Apart from Noel Roche, name the other two Clare players to play International Rules football?

357 Name the only Clare player to play in Munster hurling and football finals in the last 20 years?

358 Who managed Clare to the 1986 Munster hurling final?

359 How many All-Ireland minor football finals have Clare appeared in?

360 Name the father and son who played in Munster hurling finals in 1967 and 2008?

HARD-LUCK STORIES

361 Name the Kilkenny hurler who missed the 2006 All-Ireland final through injury?

362 Charlie Redmond missed the 1998 All-Ireland club football final after being sent off in the semi-final. With which club did Redmond play?

363 Name the Wexford hurler who missed the 1996 All-Ireland final through injury?

364 Name the Dublin footballer who missed the 1995 All-Ireland final through injury?

365 Name the Galway footballer who missed the 2000 campaign, including the 2000 All-Ireland final and replay, after damaging his cruciate ligament?

366 Name the Tipperary player who missed the 2001 All-Ireland final through suspension after being sent off in the All-Ireland semi-final?

367 Name the Cork defender who broke his hand before the 2007 All-Ireland football final and who subsequently couldn't start that game?

368 In which year did Eoin Liston miss an All-Ireland for Kerry after he had his appendix removed?

369 Name the Donegal player who missed out on Donegal's crowning glory in 1992 after he failed a fitness test that morning?

370 The Tipperary captain Pa O'Neill was controversially dropped for the 1988 All-Ireland final, which sparked a public outcry. But with which club did O'Neill play?

371 In his first year on the Armagh panel, goalkeeper Benny Tierney missed the Ulster final because of suspension and he had to wait nearly a decade to get back to another Ulster final. Name that year he was suspended?

372 Name the Dublin footballer who missed the entire 1993 championship after being sent off in the league final against Donegal?

373 Name the former Galway underage and senior player who broke his leg three weeks before the 2007 All-Ireland club final and subsequently missed the game for Loughrea?

374 Name the Tyrone forward who got injured the week before the 1995 All-Ireland final and who subsequently missed the final?

375 Name the Galway player who missed the 1980 All-Ireland final win after breaking his collarbone in the All-Ireland semi-final?

376 Name the Tipperary defender who was dropped for the 1989 All-Ireland final because – in the aftermath of the Tony Keady affair – it emerged that he had played in the London championship without proper clearance?

377 In which year did Justin McCarthy miss the All-Ireland hurling final for Cork after getting seriously injured in a motorbike accident?

378 Name the Cork defender who tore his cruciate ligament in the Munster football final replay in 2006 and who subsequently missed the rest of the season?

379 Jimmy Keaveney was sent off in the 1979 Leinster final against Offaly and would have been eligible to line out in the All-Ireland final against Kerry if the match hadn't been brought forward a week. Why was the match brought forward?

380 He was Kerry captain in 1946 and captained them to win the Munster final, but was dropped for the All-Ireland final and lost the captaincy. He came on as a sub in the final which ended level and was set to hold his place for the final and regain the captaincy. However, he broke his ankle the week of the replay against Roscommon, missed out on captaining the team and got no All-Ireland medal. He never won an All-Ireland medal. Name him?

OUTSIDE MANAGERS

381 Paul Bealin managed which two counties in the Leinster football championship between 2005-08?

382 Name the two counties that John O'Mahony has managed outside of Mayo?

383 Name the former Antrim hurling manager who managed Down in the 2008 hurling championship?

384 Name the three counties that Mickey Moran has managed outside of Derry?

385 Name the three counties that John Maughan has managed outside of Mayo?

386 Tom Cribben – a Kildare man – managed which county in the 1999 football championship?

387 How many terms did John McIntyre serve as manager of the Offaly hurlers?

388 Frank Doherty managed the Clare footballers in 2008 but from which county does he hail?

389 Name the former Kildare football manager who also managed Offaly in the last ten years?

390 Mattie Kerrigan managed which county to a football league final in 2002?

ANSWERS PAGE 224

391 Name the former Dublin footballer and manager who managed Roscommon to the 2004 Connacht final?

392 Laois hurling manager in 2007 and 2008, Damien Fox, is a native of which county?

393 Name the three Leinster counties that Pat Roe has managed this decade?

394 Name the former Galway footballer who managed Roscommon to the 2001 Connacht title?

395 Pat Begley – father of Brian (Limerick dual player) – managed which county in the football championship this decade?

396 Cyril Farrell coached which county to a provincial final in 1992?

397 Babs Keating coached which hurling team to an All-Ireland final in the 1970s?

398 Apart from Limerick, which Munster county did Eamonn Cregan manage in the 1980s?

399 Name the former Cavan footballer who managed Longford to their first and only Leinster senior football title in 1968?

400 Prior to 2008, name the only two outside football managers to win an All-Ireland senior title?

CORK GENERAL KNOWLEDGE

401 Who captained Cork to the 1990 All-Ireland hurling title?

402 Apart from Nemo Rangers and St Finbarr's, name the other two Cork clubs to win three or more Munster club football titles?

403 The two Kieran Murphys who play with the Cork hurlers go by which nicknames?

404 In 2008, the Cork hurlers gave a walkover for the first time in the county's history. Name the team that received that walkover in the Waterford Crystal Cup?

405 In 1987, the Cork county board introduced a controversial code of conduct that advised players not to compete in other codes. Which player, who played with Cork City, left the panel before returning to win two All-Irelands?

406 Name the Cork hurler who made his championship debut in the 1986 All-Ireland final?

407 Name two of the four Cork football selectors that were ultimately forced to step down (they were eventually voted out of office by the county board) as a result of the binding arbitration decision taken which ended the Cork strike in 2008?

408 Name the forward who scored Cork's second goal in the 1993 All-Ireland final?

409 Who captained Nemo Rangers to their last All-Ireland club title in 2003?

410 Name the two brothers who won Munster hurling and football medals (separately) in 1983?

ANSWERS PAGE 224

411 Who captained Cork in the 1987 All-Ireland senior football final?

412 Willie Murphy was one of nine players to win four All-Ireland medals in a row between 1941-44 but by which nickname was he commonly known?

413 Name two of the three Corkmen who share the unique distinction of winning 12 Munster senior championship medals (in both codes)?

414 Six Cork players have won National League hurling and football medals. Five of those players have achieved that feat in the last 35 years – name four of those five?

415 Who managed UCC to the 1999 Munster club title?

416 Prior to 2008, name the only Cork father and son to play in All-Ireland football semi-finals in the last 35 years?

417 Name three of the five Cork hurling selectors who were forced to step down after the players went on strike in 2002?

418 Prior to 2008, five of the top ten scorers in Munster hurling finals were Cork men. Name four of the five?

419 Ray Cummins, Jimmy Barry-Murphy, Denis Coughlan and Brian Murphy all won All-Ireland hurling and football medals with Cork in the 1970s but name the fifth Corkman who also achieved that unique honour?

420 Name the two Cork hurlers who have won All-Stars but who haven't won an All-Ireland senior title (they both won them in the last 20 years)?

ANSWERS PAGE 224

FOOTBALL ALL-STARS

421 Name the only three brothers to win All-Stars in the same season?

422 Name the two Derry footballers selected on the 2007 All-Star football team?

423 Name the Donegal footballer who was selected corner-back in 2006?

424 Who was Wexford's first football All-Star?

425 Three of the six All-Star defenders in 2002 were from Armagh. Name two of them?

426 In which season (in the last five years) was there only three counties represented on the football All-Star team?

427 In which position did the late Cormac McAnallen win an All-Star in 2003?

428 Gabriel Irwin was selected as the goalkeeper on the 1989 side. From which county did he hail?

429 Name the only Cavan player to win an All-Star in 1997?

430 How many All-Stars did Meath's John McDermott win between 1996-99, two, three or four?

431 Name three of the four Kerry players to have six or more All-Stars?

ANSWERS PAGE 224

432 Name the only non-Kerry player with six or more All-Stars?

433 True or False? Down's Mickey Linden won only one All-Star.

434 Name the only Donegal footballer to win an All-Star in the 1980s and in the 1990s?

435 How many All-Stars did Tipperary's Declan Browne win?

436 Name the two Derry footballers to win four All-Stars?

437 Who was Tyrone's first All-Star in 1980?

438 Prior to 2008, only three players had won All-Stars even though they had never played in a provincial final in the last decade. Then all three played in a provincial final in 2008. Name two of them?

439 Prior to 2008 and since the inception of the All-Ireland qualifiers in 2001, only two players had won All-Stars even though their county didn't reach the last 12 of the championship. Name them?

440 Prior to 2008, only three Ulster goalkeepers won All-Stars. Name two of those three (they were all selected in the last 20 years)?

HURLING CAPTAINS' PARADE

441 Who captained Limerick in the 2007 All-Ireland hurling final?

442 Who captained Kilkenny to the 2006 All-Ireland title?

443 Who led Waterford to the 2007 Munster hurling title?

444 Who captained Portumna to the 2008 All-Ireland club title?

445 In which year did Stephen Frampton lead Waterford to a Munster hurling final?

446 Name the two players who lifted the trophy for Tipperary after their 2008 National League and Munster final success?

447 Who captained Clare in the 2002 All-Ireland hurling final?

448 Name the Cork captain in the 2006 All-Ireland final who subsequently retired afterwards?

449 Name the player who captained Tipperary in the 2006 Munster hurling final and who never played another senior inter-county game afterwards?

450 Name the Cork player who captained his side in the 2003 All-Ireland final and who retired afterwards?

451 In which year did Peter Barry captain Kilkenny to a National league hurling title?

ANSWERS PAGE 224

452 True or False? Jimmy Barry-Murphy captained Cork in two All-Ireland finals.

453 Liam Donoghue captained Galway in the 2005 All-Ireland final to become only the third goalkeeper in the last 50 years to captain his county in an All-Ireland senior final. Name one of the other two goalkeepers to achieve that honour?

454 In the last ten years, two sets of two brothers have captained their county in the hurling championship. Name both sets of brothers?

455 Ben O'Connor captained Cork to the 2004 All-Ireland title but in which other year did O'Connor captain Cork?

456 Gary Hanniffy captained Birr to an All-Ireland club title in which year?

457 DJ Carey captained Kilkenny in the 2003 National League final but name the player (nominated by his club as Kilkenny captain) who lifted the trophy?

458 Name the hurler who captained Birr to the 1995 All-Ireland club hurling title and who captained Offaly to the All-Ireland senior final in the same season?

459 Who captained Tipperary to the 1989 All-Ireland title?

460 Name the only hurler to captain his club and county to All-Ireland honours in the same season (he managed it in the last ten seasons)?

ANSWERS PAGE 224

DERRY GENERAL KNOWLEDGE

461 Name the former Armagh All-Ireland winning trainer who joined the Derry senior football backroom team in 2008?

462 Which county did Derry defeat in the 1989 All-Ireland minor football final?

463 Who managed Derry to the 2002 All-Ireland minor title?

464 The father of Derry hurlers Liam and Kevin Hinphey, Liam senior, hails from which county?

465 Name the three sides Derry defeated in their four National football league final wins between 1992-2000?

466 True or False? A Derry player has never captained a Sigerson Cup winning team.

467 Who did Dungiven defeat in the 1997 Ulster club football final?

468 Name the Derry goalkeeper who exchanged words with referee Michael Curley in the aftermath of Derry's drawn National League final in 2000 and who was subsequently suspended for the replay?

469 Name the goalkeeper who replaced the above player in that replay?

470 Name the current inter-county manager who managed The Loup to the 2003 Ulster club title?

ANSWERS PAGE 225

471 Who captained Bellaghy in the 1995 All-Ireland club football final?

472 In which year did Derry last win an Ulster minor hurling title – 1997, 1999 or 2001?

473 Who captained Derry to the 2002 All-Ireland minor football title?

474 Name the two football All-Stars who won Ulster hurling titles in 2000 and 2001?

475 How many Ulster club hurling finals did Lavey contest in the 1990s?

476 Who captained Derry to the 1997 All-Ireland U-21 title?

477 Who managed Derry to their first Ulster senior hurling title in 2000?

478 Name the player who captained his club in Ulster club football and hurling finals in the last ten years?

479 Name the three players from Derry's All-Ireland winning senior football team of 1993 that also represented Ulster in Railway Cup hurling?

480 Name the renowned Derry footballer who captained St Pat's Maghera to the All-Ireland Colleges title in 1995 and who was also honoured as an Ulster Colleges hurling All-Star that same year?

ANSWERS PAGE 225

PLAYERS WHO CAME OUT OF RETIREMENT OR WHO MADE NOTABLE COMEBACKS

481 Name the Galway player who came out of retirement in 2008 after one season?

482 Name the Armagh All-Ireland winning forward from 2002 who retired after the 2004 championship but who returned to play in the 2007 championship?

483 Name the Waterford defender who won a Munster medal in 2002, retired after the 2003 championship and who returned to play full-back in the 2005 championship?

484 Name the Donegal forward who retired after the 2006 championship but who returned to win a National League with the county in 2007?

485 DJ Carey sensationally first announced his retirement in 1998 and he played his last championship game for Kilkenny in 2005. But which season in between those years did Carey only return to the panel for the All-Ireland semi-final, subsequently winning an All-Star on the back of only two performances?

486 Brian Corcoran won All-Ireland medals in 2004 and 2005 before retiring after the 2006 All-Ireland final. But which season did Corcoran sensationally first announce his retirement from the game?

ANSWERS PAGE 225

487 Name the Wexford forward who sensationally came out of retirement at short notice to play a part as a substitute in the 2001 drawn and replayed All-Ireland hurling semi-finals?

488 Name the only inter-county manager to come out of retirement and play in the championship in the last ten years?

489 Name the Galway footballer who came out of retirement to play in the 2006 and 2007 championship?

490 Name the former Meath All-Ireland winner and All-Star who retired after the 2005 championship before returning for the 2007 and 2008 championships?

491 Name the Dublin footballer who returned to the Dublin football team in 1974 and who subsequently went on to win three All-Irelands?

492 Name the Cork defender who came out of retirement in 1992 and who played in that year's All-Ireland hurling final?

493 Name the Armagh defender who was dropped from the squad after the 2006 championship for one season but who returned to play in the 2008 championship?

494 Name the Cork footballer who played in the 1993 All-Ireland football final and who was retired by Larry Tompkins in 2003 before coming back to play in the 2004 championship under Billy Morgan?

ANSWERS PAGE 225

495 Name the Fermanagh goalkeeper who was dropped in 2005 and who was out of the county squad before returning for the 2008 championship and lining out in that year's Ulster final?

496 He won seven All-Ireland medals with Kerry but retired in 1990. However, he came out of retirement in 1993 to play in that year's Munster final. Name him?

497 Name the Cork defender who went to the US in 1980 but who returned and played in the 1982 All-Ireland hurling final?

498 Name the legendary Kerry player who retired after the 1966 championship but who returned for the 1968 Munster championship and played for six more years?

499 Name the Cork hurling goalkeeper who had never played championship before but who came out of retirement in 1952 to win three All-Ireland senior medals in a row?

500 Kerry's Mick O'Dwyer retired in 1966 after two leg-breaks before returning for a past v present match in 1968, after which he resurrected his inter-county career, winning All-Ireland medals in 1969 and 1970. In which year did O'Dwyer finally play his last championship match for Kerry?

ANSWERS PAGE 225

GENERAL KNOWLEDGE

501 Kilkenny footballers re-entered the National Football League in 2008 for the first time since what year – 1995, 1999 or 2002?

502 Moorefield played which Longford club over three games during the 2007 Leinster club football championship?

503 Outside of Dublin, which county had two teams representing them in the 2007 National hurling league?

504 The Tipperary football manager in 2008, John Evans, led which club to All-Ireland success in the last 15 years?

505 Brendan Cummins plays club hurling with Ballybacon-Grange but with which club does he play football?

506 Name the two brothers who were sent off in a provincial senior football final in 2008?

507 Name the player who won two All-Ireland club hurling medals with Portumna and who also played in the 2001 All-Ireland hurling final with Tipperary?

508 Wexford reached Leinster senior hurling and football finals in 2008 but apart from Cork, name the last county to contest provincial senior finals in both codes in the same season?

509 Niall Corcoran, who played with Dublin hurlers in the 2008 senior championship, won an All-Ireland minor medal with which county?

ANSWERS PAGE 225

510 In the 1997 All-Ireland final, Maurice Fitzgerald accidentally broke the leg of the Kerry corner-forward. Name him?

511 Name the Labour Relations Committee Chairman who delivered the binding arbitration ruling which ultimately ended the Cork players strike in 2008?

512 Name the former Clare hurler who managed Loughrea to the 2007 All-Ireland club hurling final?

513 Which county won the 2008 Connacht U-21 football title?

514 Name the Galway midfielder who captained the county to the 2003 Connacht title?

515 In which year was the blood-sub rule first introduced – 2000, 2001 or 2002?

516 Only two counties have managed to win All-Ireland senior and minor football All-Irelands in the same year. Name them?

517 Name the two footballers who played in the 2007 football championship and who managed teams in the 2008 championship?

518 GAA President Nickey Brennan managed the Kilkenny U-21 hurlers to an All-Ireland U-21 hurling final in which year – 1990, 1993 or 1994?

519 During Joe Kernan's six-year stint as Armagh manager, only one team outside of Ulster beat Armagh in the championship. Name the team and the year?

520 Name the only hurler in the last ten years to captain a team and manage a team in an All-Ireland semi-final?

DONEGAL GENERAL KNOWLEDGE

521 Who scored Donegal's only goal in the 2002 Ulster football final?

522 Name the two brothers who played for Donegal in the 2008 football championship?

523 Name the young goalkeeper who played in the 2005 Ulster championship against Armagh, a day before his Leaving Certificate exams?

524 Who succeeded Brian McEniff as Donegal manager in 1995?

525 Prior to 2008, name the only Donegal club to win a game in the Ulster club championship in the last ten years?

526 Name the two Donegal players to captain Sigerson Cup winning teams in the last ten years?

527 Colm McFadden won a Sigerson Cup title with which college in the last ten years?

528 How many Ulster titles did Martin Carney win with Donegal before transferring to Mayo?

529 Which former Donegal All-Ireland winner and All-Star coached IT Sligo to their first Sigerson Cup title in 2002?

530 The Setanta hurling club is situated in which Donegal village?

ANSWERS PAGE 225

531 Name the only Donegal club to win an Ulster club football title?

532 The cup for the Donegal senior football championship was presented by which Donegal newspaper?

533 Killybegs, one of only two Donegal clubs to contest an Ulster club football final, made their lone provincial final appearance in which year – 1989, 1990 or 1991?

534 Name the Donegal player who was vice-captain on the Irish International Rules squad in 1990?

535 Prior to Donegal's defeat to Derry in the 2008 Ulster championship, when was the last time Donegal lost a championship match in Ballybofey?

536 Name the former and 2008 Irish Olympic Games Chef d'Equipe who trained the Donegal footballers in 2000?

537 In the 1996 Ulster senior championship, Donegal were beaten by two points by Down but what controversial incident happened in that game over the only goal in the match?

538 Name the only Donegal player to captain Ulster to Interprovincial success (he managed it in the last 15 years)?

539 When Donegal played Limerick in the 1923 All-Ireland hurling semi-final, it was the first time in a GAA game that two teams did what?

540 Name the first Donegal man to win an All-Ireland senior football medal?

ANSWERS PAGE 225

FOOTBALL'S EVOLUTION THROUGH THE LAST 65 YEARS

541 In 1946, Antrim arrived in Croke Park for an All-Ireland semi-final with a fancy hand-passing game but were rough-housed by Kerry, masters of catch-and-kick conservatism. That Antrim team never came back but how many Ulster titles have Antrim won since that year – one, two or three?

542 In the 1955 All-Ireland final against Kerry, Dublin arrived in an All-Ireland final with off-the-ball runners and the original roving full-forward. That full-forward went on to become a famous name in Dublin GAA folklore. Name him?

543 True or False? Down's eight-point win over Kerry in 1960 was the biggest defeat Kerry ever suffered in an All-Ireland final.

544 Down played Kerry on three occasions during the 1960s in the championship, 1960, 1961 and 1968. How many of those games did Down win?

545 Name the full-back who captained Dublin to the 1974 All-Ireland title?

546 Mickey Ned O'Sullivan captained Kerry in the 1975 All-Ireland final but who was presented with the Sam Maguire after Kerry's victory?

547 Charlie Nelligan came on as a substitute in the 1976 All-Ireland final and went on to win seven All-Ireland medals but who did he replace as goalkeeper in that final?

ANSWERS PAGE 225

548 Kevin Heffernan managed Dublin for most of the 1970s but in that decade, which All-Ireland winning year for Dublin was Heffernan not manager (he had stepped down for that season)?

549 How many All-Irelands did Kerry and Dublin share between them from 1974 to 1986?

550 How many All-Ireland finals did Meath and Cork contest against each other between 1987 and 1990 (including replays)?

551 Donegal won the 1992 All-Ireland title with a defined short-passing game. In the 1992 All-Ireland football final against Dublin, the Donegal full-back never kicked the ball once. Name him?

552 Which two counties did Down defeat in the 1991 and 1994 All-Ireland semi-finals?

553 Who refereed the highly controversial All-Ireland football final replay in 1996 between Meath and Mayo?

554 Who scored Galway's goal in the 1998 All-Ireland final?

555 The Kildare side of the late 1990s were the first real advocates of the blanket defence in the modern game but how many Leinster finals did they contest between 1997-2000 (including replays)?

ANSWERS PAGE 225

556 In the late 1990s and early 2000s, Armagh set a new template for football with blanket defending, hitting on the counter-attack and playing long diagonal balls into their full-forward line. They fused Crossmaglen's new template and the coaching methods practised in Queens University together to take the game to a new level. Name that legendary Queens coach who many of those Armagh players trained under?

557 Name the priest who acted as a selector with Mickey Harte's Tyrone All-Ireland winning teams in 2003 and 2005?

558 Name the former member of the Kerry four-in-a-row winning team from 1978-81 who was a selector with the Kerry All-Ireland winning teams from 2004 and 2006?

559 True or False? Peter Canavan came off as a substitute before coming back on again in both the 2003 and 2005 All-Ireland finals.

560 How many goals did Kieran Donaghy score for Kerry in the 2006 and 2007 All-Ireland finals?

ANSWERS PAGE 225

OUTSTANDING HURLERS AND FOOTBALLERS WHO NEVER WON AN ALL-IRELAND SENIOR MEDAL WITH THEIR COUNTY

561 Possibly the greatest player never to win an All-Ireland football medal was a Sligo man who scored 36-1,158 during his career, winning a Connacht title in 1975. Name him?

562 On the GAA's Hurling Team of the Century Who Have Never Won an All-Ireland (1984), the centre-back was a Clare-man who lost Munster hurling finals in 1977, 1978, 1981 and 1986. Name him?

563 Name the current commander of the Irish Armed Forces who played in an All-Ireland final in 1980?

564 Tyrone's Frank McGuigan had his career tragically cut short after an accident in which year – 1984, 1985 or 1986?

565 How many All-Ireland finals did Cork's Ciaran O'Sullivan play in during his career?

566 Seanie Duggan was the goalkeeper selected on the GAA's Hurling Team of the Century Who Have Never Won an All-Ireland. With which county did he play?

567 Name the former Mayo footballer, who played in the 1989 All-Ireland final, whose son played in the 2004 and 2006 All-Ireland finals for Mayo?

ANSWERS PAGE 225

568 Antrim's only representative on the GAA's Hurling Team of the Century Who Have Never Won an All-Ireland had a son who played in the 1989 All-Ireland hurling final for Antrim. Name that representative?

569 Clare's Jimmy Smyth played on how many successful Railway Cup teams for Munster – 8, 9 or 10?

570 Limerick's Ciaran Carey played in an All-Ireland club hurling final in 1991 with which club?

571 Name the former Kildare captain who managed the county U-21s to the 2008 All-Ireland final?

572 Former Limerick goalkeeper Tommy Quaid played for the county for 18 years but he won his sole All-Star in which year – 1980, 1987 or 1992?

573 Mayo's David Brady first appeared in an All-Ireland club final for Ballina Stephenites in which year?

574 Ger Loughnane played in his last Munster final for Clare in which year?

575 Tipperary's Declan Browne won his first All-Star in which season?

576 Terence 'Sambo' McNaughton played with which Antrim club?

577 In how many All-Ireland club finals did Joe Kavanagh play with Nemo Rangers?

ANSWERS PAGE 225

578 Name the Armagh player who won six Railway Cups but who never even won an Ulster medal, having retired the year before Armagh won the Ulster title in 1999?

579 In the 1970 All-Ireland final, four Quigley brothers lined out for Wexford – Dan, Martin, Pat and John. Three of those brothers won All-Irelands, but which one played for Wexford for almost 20 years, never winning an All-Ireland?

580 On the GAA's Football Team of the Century Who Have Never Won an All-Ireland, there was a player selected who subsequently went on to win an All-Ireland. Name him?

ANSWERS PAGE 225

DOWN GENERAL KNOWLEDGE

581 Which county did Down defeat in both the 1999 and 2005 All-Ireland minor football finals?

582 True or False? Although Ballycran, Ballygalget and Portaferry are the three dominant hurling clubs in Down, another club outside the Ards peninsula has won the most Down senior hurling titles.

583 Which county did Down defeat to win the 2008 Dr McKenna Cup title?

584 Down's first hurling All-Star replacement was a Ballygalget man. Name him?

585 Name the father who won an All-Ireland football medal in 1968 and the son who played in the 2008 championship?

586 Down have won six Ulster U-21 football titles and one All-Ireland U-21 title but how many All-Ireland U-21 finals have they appeared in – two, three or four?

587 Burren played in eight Ulster club finals in the 1980s but how many Ulster titles did they win?

588 Who defeated Bryansford in the first ever All-Ireland club final in 1971?

589 Name the five men who have captained Down to the Sam Maguire?

590 Along with Bryansford, Burren and Mayobridge, name the only other Down club to reach an Ulster club football final?

591 Who managed Ballygalget to the 2005 Ulster club hurling title?

592 Who captained Down to the 2005 All-Ireland minor football title?

593 Prior to 2008, name the only other Down club apart from Ballygalget to win an Ulster club hurling title?

594 Who captained Down to the 1999 All-Ireland minor football title?

595 Name the three Down brothers who played in the 2008 Ulster senior hurling final?

596 Who scored Down's only goal in the 1991 All-Ireland football final?

597 Who captained Down to their first Ulster hurling title in 1992?

598 Two players from the Down All-Ireland winning team of 1991 have sons who have played championship football for Down. Name the fathers and the sons?

599 When Down were going for three All-Ireland football titles in a row in 1962, who defeated them in that year's Ulster final by ten points?

600 Name the only Down hurler nominated for an All-Star on four occasions?

ANSWERS PAGE 226

FOOTBALL CAPTAINS' PARADE

601 Who captained Cork in the 2007 All-Ireland football final?

602 Who captained Kildare in the 1998 All-Ireland football final?

603 Who captained Tyrone to the 2007 Ulster football title?

604 Who captained Derry to the 2008 National Football league title?

605 James Masters captained Cork to an All-Ireland minor title in which season?

606 Who captained Dublin to the 2007 Leinster football title?

607 Who captained St Vincent's to the 2008 All-Ireland club football title?

608 Who captained Kerry in the 2002 All-Ireland final?

609 Who captained Armagh to their first Ulster football title in 17 years in 1999?

610 Who captained Dublin to the 1983 All-Ireland title?

611 Who captained Cork to the 2008 Munster senior football title?

612 Who captained Offaly to the famous 1982 All-Ireland title?

ANSWERS PAGE 226

613 Wexford hurling manager in 2008, John Meyler, captained which club to an All-Ireland club football title in 1987?

614 Name the Ballina Stephenites player who led the club to their first All-Ireland title in 2005?

615 Who is the last player to captain successive National League winning teams?

616 Who captained Westmeath to their historic first Leinster senior football title in 2004?

617 Prior to 2008, who was the last player to captain his county to an All-Ireland U-21 and All-Ireland senior title?

618 Apart from Declan O'Sullivan, name the last player to captain successive All-Ireland winning senior football teams?

619 Prior to 2008, name the last player to captain his county in All-Ireland minor and senior football finals (it was in the last 15 years)?

620 Name the player who captained his club to provincial club titles almost a decade apart – between 1998 and 2008?

HURLERS WHO HAVE PLAYED IN ALL-IRELAND FINALS OVER THE LAST 20 YEARS

Match the county to the player

621 Peter Lawlor

622 Conor Phelan

623 Pat O'Connor

624 Ollie Kilkenny

625 John Heffernan

626 Aidan McCarry

627 Michael O'Halloran

628 Sean O'Gorman

629 Darren Hanniffy

630 Jimmy Coogan

631 Brian Higgins

632 Joe Hayes

633 Kevin Hayes

634 Terence Donnelly

635 Joe O'Connor

636 Gerry Burke

637 David Quirke

638 Leo O'Connor

639 Paul Finn

640 Gearóid Considine

ANSWERS PAGE 226

DUBLIN GENERAL KNOWLEDGE

641 Prior to 2008, name the two Dublin brothers to play International Rules?

642 Name the player who played in Dublin county senior football finals with two different clubs in the last five years?

643 Name the former Kilkenny player and manager who managed the Dublin hurlers at the outset of this decade?

644 True or False? Prior to 2008, every time that a Dublin club (outside of UCD) has won an All-Ireland club title, the county have subsequently gone on to win the All-Ireland senior title?

645 Who managed the Dublin hurlers to their last Leinster senior final appearance in 1991?

646 Prior to 2008, in which season since the arrival of the qualifier system, did Dublin beat only Leinster teams en route to an All-Ireland football semi-final?

647 Dublin defeated Longford in the 2008 O'Byrne Cup final after scoring two goals in the dying minutes. Name the Dublin forward who scored those two goals?

648 Name the two counties that defeated Dublin in the 2005 and 2007 All-Ireland minor hurling semi-finals?

649 Who captained Dublin to the 2002 Leinster title?

ANSWERS PAGE 226

650 Who won Dublin's first hurling All-Star award?

651 Prior to 2008, when was the last time that Dublin beat Kerry in the All-Ireland senior football championship?

652 Who managed Dublin to the 2007 Leinster minor hurling title?

653 Prior to 2008, three Dublin footballers had won four All-Stars. Name two of them?

654 Kathleen Mills holds the record number of All-Ireland Camogie medals with 15 but name the Dublin player who holds the second highest number of All-Ireland Camogie medals with 13?

655 In the first-half of the 1995 All-Ireland football final, Dublin scored points from four different place-kickers. Name three of them?

656 Prior to 2008, Dublin clubs had the best record in the Leinster club football championship, making 22 Leinster final appearances, winning 13 titles. Name six of the eight clubs to win titles?

657 Name the Dublin player who won an All-Ireland minor medal as a goalkeeper in 1982 and an All-Ireland senior medal as a corner-forward in 1983?

658 Who was Dublin's only All-Star footballer in 2001?

ANSWERS PAGE 226

659 Name the only Dublin player to captain Leinster to an Interprovincial (formerly Railway Cup) hurling title?

660 Name the father and son who won All-Ireland senior football medals in 1963 and 1995 with Dublin?

ANSWERS PAGE 226

GENERAL KNOWLEDGE

661 Wexford's first hurling All-Star winner in 1972 has had two sons on the Wexford senior hurling team over the last number of years. Name him?

662 Name the five Galway clubs to have reached All-Ireland club hurling finals in the last ten years?

663 Kieran McGeeney played his last game for Armagh in the 2007 championship. Who defeated Armagh that day?

664 Name the former All-Ireland winning hurling manager who was the Dublin Director of Hurling for two years in 2002 and 2003?

665 Name the Galway All-Ireland winner from 1998 who played with Kildare in the 2006 football championship?

666 In which year did Liam Hayes captain Meath in an All-Ireland senior football final?

667 With which club does Limerick's Mark Foley play?

668 Clonkill won the All-Ireland Intermediate club hurling title in 2008 to secure an All-Ireland hurling title for which county for the first time?

669 Prior to 2008, name the last footballer to captain his county to a National League title and an All-Ireland title in the same season?

670 Name the only player to have won an All-Ireland senior hurling medal and to have also played International Rules in the last ten years?

671 Name the hurling goalkeeper who won three All-Ireland Poc Fada titles in four years between 2004-07?

672 The Mayo hurling coach/selector in 2008 was a double All-Ireland winner from 1987-'88 who also won five All-Stars. Name him?

673 In the 2007 Kerry club hurling final between Lixnaw and Kilmoyley, the teams were managed by a former All-Ireland winning captain and a former All-Ireland winning manager from the last 15 years. Name them?

674 In which year was the decision taken at GAA Congress to amend Rule 42 to allow playing rugby and soccer internationals at Croke Park?

675 The first ever midweek championship game was played between which counties in the last five years?

676 Kieran O'Connor and Pearse O'Neill – who played in the 2007 All-Ireland football final for Cork – are from a club in the stronghold hurling division of east Cork. Name the club?

677 Name the Cork hurling captain over the last five years who played in the 2000 All-Ireland minor hurling final as a goalkeeper and the 2000 All-Ireland minor football final as a midfielder?

678 Name the Cork dual player who played hurling and football championship matches on the same day in 2002?

679 Name three of the five counties to play in Division One and Division Two National League finals in the last ten years?

680 Name the only set of twins to play International Rules football?

PLAYERS WHO MADE NOTABLE POSITIONAL SWITCHES

681 In his first game at full-forward in the 2006 championship, Kieran Donaghy set up three goals against which county?

682 Name the Waterford player who scored 0-7 from play as a forward in the 2002 Munster final but who subsequently won two more Munster titles as a defender?

683 Brian Corcoran won two All-Irelands at full-forward but from which position did he win Hurler of the Year in 1999?

684 Name the Monaghan full-back who was converted from full-back to full-forward in the 2007 championship?

685 Ollie Canning won two All-Stars as a corner-back but he was also a forward. In the 1999 drawn All-Ireland quarter-final, he was straight through on goal and a goal would have put the game out of sight but his rocket of a shot hit the crossbar. Against which county did Galway play in that game?

686 True or False? Brian Begley made his name as a full-forward but he made his championship debut at full-back.

687 Name the Waterford player who played centre-forward in the 2001 championship and who won an All-Star as a half-back a year later?

688 Name the Tipperary player who won an All-Star as a half-back in 2000 and who won an All-Ireland senior medal as a forward a year later?

689 Name the Wexford hurler who scored the decisive goal in the 2004 Leinster hurling semi-final from corner-forward but who was the county's best player in the 2008 drawn Leinster semi-final against Dublin from wing-back?

690 Name the Kerry corner-forward from the 2007 All-Ireland final who played as a goalkeeper with the Kerry minors in 2003?

691 True or False? The legendary Tipperary forward Jimmy Doyle played his last championship match as a goalkeeper.

692 Name the Tipperary forward who scored five points from play in the 1991 All-Ireland final and who won Hurler of the Year in the same season but who also played at corner-back in the 1984 Munster final?

693 Name the Meath footballer who had scored 14 championship goals prior to the 2008 championship but who scored his first goal in the 1994 Leinster final from wing-back?

694 In which year did Tommy Dunne play most of his championship games for Tipperary at centre-back?

695 Name the Offaly full-back who won an All-Ireland in 1981 and who ended his career at full-forward?

696 Name the Limerick hurler who played corner-forward in the 1994 and 1996 All-Ireland finals and who ended up playing the last seven years of his career at full-back?

ANSWERS PAGE 227

697 Name the former Clare All-Star hurling defender who started the 2004 championship at full-forward?

698 Name the player who got man of the match from centre-back in the 1981 All-Ireland hurling final against Galway and who finished his career at centre-forward in the 1988 All-Ireland semi-final against the same opposition?

699 Name the Antrim hurler who began his career as a forward but who played corner-back in the 1989 All-Ireland final?

700 Name the Offaly forward who won All-Ireland medals in 1994 and 1998 but who played in both the All-Ireland minor and U-21 hurling finals as a goalkeeper in 1989?

ANSWERS PAGE 227

FERMANAGH GENERAL KNOWLEDGE

701 Who was selected as Fermanagh's first football All-Star?

702 Name the Fermanagh goalkeeper who was selected as Young Footballer of the Year in 2004?

703 Name the father and two sons who were involved with Fermanagh in the 1990s as manager and players?

704 Name the former All-Ireland medal winner with Meath who managed Fermanagh in the mid 1990s?

705 In which year did Raymond Gallagher score a goal on his senior championship debut while he was still a minor?

706 Cormac McAdam, who played in goals for Fermanagh in the 1990s, went by what nickname?

707 How many MacRory Cup titles did St Michael's Enniskillen win between 1999 and 2002 – one, two or three?

708 Name the Fermanagh hurler who played in the 2008 championship and who was a member of Ulster Railway Cup squads in the 1990s?

709 Who was the first Fermanagh man to captain Ulster to a Railway Cup in 1980?

710 Name the Fermanagh player who was the top scorer in the 2000 Sigerson Cup final?

ANSWERS PAGE 227

711 In which two years did Fermanagh win the All-Ireland B Football title?

712 Liam McBarron famously travelled back to Fermanagh via helicopter to get married in 2004 after Fermanagh's Round 4 qualifier win against which county?

713 Which county defeated Fermanagh in successive All-Ireland U-21 finals in 1970 and 1971?

714 Name the two Fermanagh footballers who won an Interprovincial title with Ulster in 2007?

715 Tom Walsh, Fermanagh hurling manager in 2008, won an All-Ireland minor hurling medal with which county?

716 Name the Fermanagh man who managed the county to the 1982 Ulster senior football final and also name his son, who played in the 2008 Ulster final?

717 Name the sponsor of the Fermanagh footballers, who has now sponsored the county teams since 1991?

718 Name the only Fermanagh player to captain a Sigerson Cup winning team (he managed it in the last 15 years)?

719 Name the three Fermanagh players to play International Rules Football?

720 Who was the first Fermanagh player to play on a winning Railway Cup winning football team with Ulster?

ANSWERS PAGE 227

LAST TITLE WON AS A MANAGER

721 What was the last title won by Jack O'Connor as manager of Kerry?

722 What was the last title won by Joe Kernan as manager of Armagh?

723 What was the last title won by Ger Loughnane when he was manager of Clare?

724 What trophy did John Allen last win with Cork before he stepped down as manager?

725 Name the last trophy won by John Maughan as manager of Mayo?

726 Name the last trophy won by John O'Mahony as manager of Galway?

727 Name the last championship title that Billy Morgan won with Cork before he departed the managerial position in 2007?

728 What was the last title Tom Ryan won when he was manager of Limerick?

729 What was the last title Conor Hayes won as manager of Galway before he departed in 2006?

730 What was the last title Nicky English won as manager of Tipperary?

ANSWERS PAGE 227

731 Name the last inter-county competition won by the late Eamonn Coleman as manager?

732 What was the last senior hurling trophy won by Mattie Murphy while he was manager of Galway?

733 Name the last championship won by Jimmy Barry-Murphy before he stepped down as Cork manager?

734 Name the last trophy won by the late Ollie Walsh as Kilkenny manager?

735 What was the last trophy won by Pete McGrath as manager of Down?

736 What was the last championship title won by Eugene McGee when he was manager of Offaly?

737 What was the last trophy won by Kevin Heffernan as manager/coach of Dublin?

738 Name the last trophy won by Cyril Farrell as manager of Galway?

739 Which title did Sean Boylan last win before he stepped down as Meath manager?

740 What was the last trophy Babs Keating won as a senior inter-county manager?

ANSWERS PAGE 227

OUTSTANDING INDIVIDUAL HURLING AND FOOTBALL SCORING PERFORMANCES OVER THE LAST 30 YEARS

741 Eoin Kelly scored 0-14 in the 2006 Munster hurling quarter-final against which county?

742 Name the Offaly player who scored 0-16 in the 2008 Leinster hurling quarter-final against Laois?

743 Name the Roscommon forward who scored 0-13 in the qualifiers against Kildare in 2003?

744 Matty Forde scored 2-10 for Wexford against which county in the 2004 qualifiers?

745 Which Waterford player scored 0-8 from play against Clare in the 2008 Munster hurling quarter-final?

746 Name the Armagh player who hit 0-10 in the 2005 National League final?

747 Name the player who hit 0-13 in the 2004 All-Ireland hurling semi-final?

748 Name the player who hit 0-14 in the 2007 All-Ireland hurling semi-final?

749 In which year did Paul Flynn score 0-12 in a Munster semi-final?

ANSWERS PAGE 227

750 In which year's championship did Henry Shefflin hit 2-11 against Offaly?

751 Name the only player to score 1-14 (a total of 17 points) in an All-Ireland hurling semi-final in the last 30 years?

752 Name the Galway player who hit 2-11 against Derry in the 2001 All-Ireland hurling quarter-final?

753 Name the player who scored 2-9 in a Munster hurling semi-final in 2006?

754 In which year did Matt Connor score 2-9 against Kerry in the football championship?

755 Name the Kilkenny hurler who hit eight points from play in the 2000 All-Ireland semi-final against Galway?

756 Which player hit 0-12 against Meath in the 2006 Leinster football quarter-final?

757 Which player holds the record individual score in an Ulster football final with 2-7?

758 Name the Derry hurler who hit 0-15 against Kerry in an All-Ireland qualifier in 2003?

759 Name the Kilkenny player who hit eight points from play in the 1979 Leinster hurling final against Wexford?

760 Name the Limerick hurler who hit nine points from play in the 1955 Munster final against Clare?

ANSWERS PAGE 227

GALWAY GENERAL KNOWLEDGE

761 Who captained Galway in the 2008 National league final?

762 In which (championship) year did John O'Mahony first take over the Galway footballers?

763 Who are the only Galway school to win an All-Ireland Colleges hurling title?

764 Who captained Galway to their first All-Ireland ladies' senior football title in 2004?

765 In how many championship seasons has Padraig Joyce captained Galway – three, four or five?

766 Who captained Galway to their first All-Ireland Camogie title in 1996?

767 Name the Galway player to win All-Ireland U-21 football medals on the field of play in 2002 and 2005?

768 Name the two sets of Galway brothers to have won hurling All-Stars?

769 Name the Sarsfields player who captained Galway in the 1993 All-Ireland hurling final?

770 The film-maker Pat Comer won county senior football medals with which two clubs in the 1990s?

ANSWERS PAGE 227

771 Only one Galway referee has taken charge of an All-Ireland football final in the last 50 years. Name him (he refereed the 1999 final)?

772 Name the player who played in the senior hurling championship for Galway in 2007, 12 years after making his inter-county championship debut?

773 Gary Fahey captained Galway to the 2001 All-Ireland football title but name the Galway player who began that season as captain?

774 Former Offaly manager, John McIntyre, managed which Galway club to an All-Ireland club final in the last 15 years?

775 In which year did Galway first compete in the Munster hurling championship – 1958, 1959 or 1960?

776 Name the two Galway players selected on the GAA's Centenary Hurling Team, comprising players who never won All-Ireland senior medals?

777 Who managed Galway to the 1995 Connacht football title?

778 Only three hurlers have played in Interprovincial finals in three different decades. One is a Galway man. Name him?

779 Name the two Galway brothers who played in All-Ireland senior hurling and football finals (separately) in the 1980s?

780 Although Conor Hayes was Galway manager in 2004, name the two Galway men who led Connacht to the Interprovincial title that season?

TRADITIONAL AND NEW RIVALRIES

781 Armagh and Donegal met in the football championship seven times between 2002 and 2007 but how many of those games did Donegal win – one, two or three?

782 Clare and Limerick met in the Munster hurling championship for four years in a row between 1993–96 but how many of those games were Munster finals?

783 True or False? Kilkenny and Tipperary met eight times in the hurling championship over 80 years in the last century and Kilkenny only won one of those games.

784 Name the Tipperary substitute who scored two goals in extra-time of the epic 1987 Munster hurling final replay against Cork?

785 Who scored the winning point for Dublin in injury time of the 1993 Leinster semi-final against Meath?

786 Mayo defeated Galway in the 1999 Connacht final to relieve them of their provincial and All-Ireland titles. Who managed Mayo that day?

787 Waterford-Cork is the first great hurling rivalry of the 21st century, having met nine times in the championship between 2002 and 2007. Which county leads the way in wins from those games?

ANSWERS PAGE 228

788 Cavan-Monaghan have a huge traditional rivalry but they've only met twice in the Ulster championship in the last 15 years. In which of those years did they meet in an Ulster semi-final?

789 Name the brothers who played for Westmeath in the 1970s and whose sons (with the same names), while living only a few miles apart, have played for different counties over the last decade?

790 When Wexford defeated Kilkenny in the 1984 Leinster semi-final, thus denying Kilkenny a chance to win three All-Irelands in a row, name the Wexford player who scored a late goal to win the match?

791 In the 1996 drawn Munster hurling final, Limerick came from ten points down to draw with Tipperary. Name the Limerick player who scored the equaliser?

792 Prior to 2000, a certain county had only beaten Donegal once in the history of the championship. However, on seven occasions between 2000 and 2007, Donegal only won two of those clashes. Name that county (apart from Armagh)?

793 Clare and Tipperary met eight times in the hurling championship between 1997 and 2003 with Clare winning four of those clashes and drawing one. But in which of those three years did Tipperary win on three successive occasions?

ANSWERS PAGE 228

794 Name the club situated right on the Tyrone-Armagh border which supplied three players to the Tyrone starting team which defeated Armagh in the 2003 All-Ireland final?

795 Offaly contested every Leinster final in the 1980s but in how many of those finals did they beat Kilkenny – two, three or four?

796 Name the Laois club that used to play in the Carlow championship?

797 Half of Newry is situated in Down and the other half is in Armagh because which river splits the town?

798 Name the famous Derry club, whose pitch lies within the Tyrone border?

799 Name the referee who took charge of the infamous Galway-Tipperary All-Ireland hurling semi-final in 1989?

800 There is a club on the Cork-Kerry border which, although the town and pitch are situated within Cork, the parish extends into Kerry. Since they draw half of their players from Kerry, as part of an agreement with the Kerry county board, players good enough to play for the county play with Kerry. Name the club?

ANSWERS PAGE 228

GENERAL KNOWLEDGE

801 Name the former Galway double All-Ireland winning footballer who released his autobiography in Irish in 2007?

802 Name the club that lost five County Antrim hurling finals in a row between 2003 and 2007?

803 Name the former Armagh All-Ireland medal winner from 2002 who won a Meath county football title with Seneschalstown in 2007?

804 Pat Kelly and Brian Maloney won an All-Ireland club title with St Vincent's in 2008 but with which county had they both played in an All-Ireland final in the previous five years?

805 What year did Cork last contest a National hurling league final?

806 Who was selected as Young Hurler of the Year in 2007?

807 Who was selected as Young Footballer of the Year in 2007?

808 In which year was the first Ulster senior football final played in Croke Park?

809 Name the player who scored goals in the All-Ireland U-21 and senior finals in 2007?

810 Name the only non-Galway player to play in the 2007 Interprovincial hurling final for Connacht?

ANSWERS PAGE 228

811 Name the Tipperary club that won the 2007 Munster club hurling title?

812 Name Tipperary's two goalscorers in the 2008 Munster hurling final?

813 Name the three former All-Ireland football winners who sang together for charity in 2007?

814 Kilkenny's Pat O'Neill was selected as man of the match in the All-Ireland hurling final in which year – 1992 or 1993?

815 Prior to 2008, only two hurlers have won Hurler of the Year in the last ten years even though their county didn't play in an All-Ireland final. Name them?

816 Who was GAA President in Centenary Year?

817 How many points did Joe Canning score from sideline cuts in the 2008 Fitzgibbon Cup final – two, three or four?

818 Who captained Kerry in the 1982 All-Ireland final when they were going for five in a row?

819 Name the hurler who captained his club to provincial club hurling titles 16 years apart?

820 The most points scored from play in a major hurling championship match (ten) were scored by which player in the 1972 All-Ireland semi-final?

ANSWERS PAGE 228

KERRY GENERAL KNOWLEDGE

821 Name the former eight-time football All-Ireland medal winner who coached the hurlers to a league final in 2006?

822 Of the eight teams who contested the National league finals (Division 1, 2, 3 and 4) in 2008, three of them were managed by Kerrymen. Name them and the counties they managed?

823 Name the Kerry footballer who was a member of the St Brendan's College backroom team, who reached the 2008 All-Ireland colleges final?

824 Name the eight-time All-Ireland football medal winner who was the Kerry team mascot for the 1962 Kerry All-Ireland champions?

825 Name the two Kerry brothers who were sent off in the 1965 All-Ireland final against Galway?

826 In which year did the three Ó Sé brothers (Darragh, Tomás and Marc) start an All-Ireland final together for the first time?

827 In which season did Tadhg Kennelly play in an All-Ireland U-21 final with Kerry?

828 True or False. A Kerry team has never won a game in the Munster club hurling championship since its start in 1971?

829 Who scored Kerry's goal in the 2008 Munster football final?

830 True or False. Sean Kelly was the first and only Kerry GAA President?

ANSWERS PAGE 228

831 In the 2006 All-Ireland minor final, three sons of men who won All-Ireland medals on the great Kerry teams between 1975-86 lined out for Kerry. Name the fathers and sons?

832 Name the Kerry player from the St Brendan's club in Ardfert who holds the remarkable distinction of playing in three Munster finals on the same day in 1956 – with the Kerry junior hurlers, junior footballers and senior footballers?

833 Name the Kerry club that won the Munster club hurling league in 2002?

834 Who captained Kerry in the 1976 All-Ireland final?

835 Name the Kerry player who holds the joint-record for the highest score recorded in an All-Ireland final over 80 minutes?

836 True or False? Kerry were the first county to defeat Clare in the National hurling league after their All-Ireland final success in 1995.

837 How many Munster senior football medals has Darragh Ó Sé won?

838 In which season in the last 30 years did Kerry only play three games to win the All-Ireland title?

839 The fastest goal in All-Ireland football final history was scored in 1962 after 34 seconds. Name the Kerry goalscorer?

840 Name the last Kerry player to win an All-Ireland colleges hurling medal (as a member of the starting 15)?

ANSWERS PAGE 228

GREAT SERVANTS OF THE LAST 20 YEARS

841 Name the Kildare footballer who made his debut in the 1992 championship and who played in the 2008 championship?

842 Name the Kerry footballer who made his debut in the 1992 Munster football final and who retired after the 2006 All-Ireland final?

843 How many championship games did Davy Fitzgerald play for Clare before retiring in 2008 – 50, 55 or 60?

844 Name the Waterford hurler who made his championship debut in 1992 and who played in the 2008 championship?

845 Name the legendary Down forward who won All-Ireland medals in 1991 and 1994 and who played in the 2004 Ulster club football final for Mayobridge?

846 Name the only Limerick footballer to play in Munster football finals in 1991 and 2003 and 2004?

847 Name the Wexford hurler who made his championship debut in 1988 and who retired after the 2003 championship, the same season he was voted Wexford Hurler of the Year?

848 Name the only Limerick player to play in All-Ireland hurling finals in 1996 and 2007?

849 In which year did Graham Geraghty play in his first Leinster senior final?

850 Name the Armagh player who captained the county in the 1992 All-Ireland minor final and in the 2008 football championship?

851 Name the Kerry footballer who played in the 1975 All-Ireland final and who retired after the 1991 All-Ireland semi-final?

852 Name the Waterford hurler who made his championship debut in 1993 and who played in the 2008 championship?

853 Name the Mayo footballer who made his championship debut in 1995 and who played in the 2008 championship?

854 Name the legendary Galway hurling forward who played in his first senior All-Ireland final in 1985 and who played his last championship match in 1999?

855 Name the Offaly player who made his championship debut in 1984 and who retired after the 2000 season?

856 Name the Carlow dual player who made his championship debut with the footballers in 1988 and who played his last championship match in 2005?

857 Name the Clare player who made his championship debut in 1995 and who played in the 2008 championship?

858 Name the Wexford footballer who made his debut in the 1993 championship and who retired after the 2007 season?

859 Name the Louth footballer who made his championship debut in 1985 and who retired in 2001?

860 Name the Down hurler who made his championship debut in 1990 and who played in the 2007 championship?

ANSWERS PAGE 228

YOUNG STARS

861 Ken McGrath made his senior championship debut with Waterford in which season as a minor?

862 Name the hurling All-Star winner from 2007 who made his championship debut in 2003 at just 17?

863 True or False? Eoin Kelly was listed as sub goalkeeper on the Tipperary senior team for the 2000 All-Ireland quarter-final against Galway but he came on as a sub and scored a point, even though he was still a minor?

864 Trevor Giles captained Meath in the 1993 All-Ireland minor final but what senior title did he win with Meath a year later?

865 Name the hurler who captained Galway to the 2000 All-Ireland minor title and who played in an All-Ireland senior final at midfield a year later?

866 Name the Laois forward who played in the 2004 Leinster football final replay, a year before captaining Knockbeg College to the All-Ireland Colleges title?

867 Name the player who captained Clare to the 1997 All-Ireland minor title and who started the All-Ireland semi-final (second replay) a year later?

868 Although Kerry defeated Waterford in the 1993 Munster championship, how many goals did Paul Flynn score that day on his championship debut?

ANSWERS PAGE 228

869 Name the player who captained Galway to the 2007 All-Ireland minor title and who made his senior championship debut against Roscommon in 2008?

870 Name the Cork footballer who played in the 1988 All-Ireland senior final even though he was only a few weeks overage for minor?

871 In which season did Niall McNamee make his senior inter-county championship debut for Offaly while he was still a minor?

872 John Leahy made his senior championship debut with Tipperary, a year after he played in an All-Ireland minor hurling final. Name the year of that minor final?

873 Brian Cody played in an All-Ireland senior final, a year after captaining the Kilkenny minors to an All-Ireland title. In which year did Cody play in that first senior final?

874 Joe Deane made his senior championship debut a year after winning an All-Ireland minor title. Which year did he make that senior debut?

875 Name the Armagh minor who made his senior championship debut in 1993, only a month after he had spearheaded St Colman's Newry to an All-Ireland Colleges title?

876 Name the Cork hurler who scored 1-1 with his first two touches on his senior championship debut against Waterford in the 2006 All-Ireland semi-final?

ANSWERS PAGE 228

877 Name the only player to win Hurler of the Year in his first season as a 19-year-old?

878 Name the Donegal footballer who played in the 2007 and 2008 championship, even though he was still a secondary student in both years?

879 Jimmy Doyle from Tipperary scored 1-8 against Kilkenny in an All-Ireland semi-final in his first year out of minor. Name the year?

880 Name the first player in history to be leveraged as a brand ambassador for two huge sporting companies before he had even made his senior inter-county debut?

KILDARE GENERAL KNOWLEDGE

881 In which year did Mick O'Dwyer first take over in Kildare (championship season)?

882 Former goalkeeper Christy Byrne made his championship debut in which year's Leinster final in the 1990s?

883 Which county did Kildare defeat in the 2008 All-Ireland U-21 semi-final?

884 Who captained Kildare to the 2004 Leinster U-21 football title?

885 In which year did Allenwood win their first county senior football title?

886 Name the selector on the Kildare U-21 team in 2008 who refereed the 2005 All-Ireland senior football final?

887 Who was Kildare's first football All-Star?

888 Who managed Kildare to the 2007 Christy Ring Cup final?

889 Who captained Kildare in the 2008 All-Ireland U-21 final?

890 Who defeated Round Towers in the 2003 Leinster club football final?

891 Name the Kildare player who won an All-Star in 1991, which was only the county's second All-Star?

ANSWERS PAGE 228

892 Which club has won the most number of Kildare county senior hurling titles, even though their last title was won in 1922?

893 Name the only two Kildare clubs to win Leinster club football titles?

894 Name the two Kildare senior hurlers who play their club hurling with Buffers Alley in Wexford?

895 How many Leinster club football finals have Sarsfields contested in the last ten years?

896 Name the former Kildare footballer who played in the 1998 All-Ireland final and who is now a successful horse trainer?

897 When Kildare and Meath played one of the games of the decade in the 1997 replayed Leinster semi-final, name the Kildare substitute who tied the scores in extra-time at 2-20 to 3-17 to take the game to a second replay?

898 Name the only Kildare GAA Ard Stiúrthóir?

899 When Bill 'Squires' Gannon captained Kildare to the 1928 All-Ireland football title, he also had the honour of becoming the first man in GAA history to do what that afternoon?

900 Name the only Kildare man to win All-Ireland senior hurling and football medals?

ANSWERS PAGE 228

FITZGIBBON AND SIGERSON CUPS

901 Which college won the Sigerson Cup in 2008?

902 Which college have won four of the last six Fitzgibbon Cups?

903 Mayo's Conor Mortimer won a Sigerson Cup medal with which college?

904 Ray McLoughney was Waterford IT's top scorer in the 2008 Fitzgibbon Cup final with a tally of 0-12. From which county does he hail?

905 Name the current Tipperary defender who was voted Player of the Fitzgibbon Tournament for two successive years in 1999 and 2000?

906 Name the Kilkenny player who played in the 2004 All-Ireland senior hurling final and who was voted Player of the Fitzgibbon Tournament for two successive years in 2003 and 2004?

907 In the last ten years, Jack Ferriter, a former All-Ireland minor winning captain, is the only player to be top scorer in two Sigerson Cup finals. With which college did he play in those Sigerson finals?

908 Which Ulster college did Down's DJ Kane captain to Sigerson glory in 1987?

909 Who were the last college to win three Sigerson titles in a row?

ANSWERS PAGE 229

910 The Tipperary footballer Declan Browne won a Fitzgibbon Cup medal as a starting forward with which college?

911 Which college won eight Fitzgibbon Cup titles in a row in the 1980s?

912 Name the Limerick player who played in Sigerson and Fitzgibbon Cup finals in the same season with UCD in 2000 and 2001?

913 Sean McMahon and Brian Lohan won Fitzgibbon Cup medals with which college in the 1990s?

914 Name the Waterford hurler who captained Waterford IT to the 2008 Fitzgibbon Cup title?

915 Which two colleges contested the Sigerson Cup semi-finals in 2008 for the first time in their history?

916 Name the Galway hurler who was selected as Player of the Tournament in the 2007 Fitzgibbon Cup, even though he was on the losing side (NUIG) in the final?

917 Name the two brothers who scored a combined total of 1-8 from play in the 2008 Fitzgibbon Cup final for Waterford IT?

918 Name the only player to captain two different colleges to Sigerson Cup titles (he achieved that feat in the last ten years)?

919 Name the three brothers who played on the UCD team which reached the 2001 Sigerson Cup final?

920 Martin McAleese, husband of Mary McAleese (Irish President) won a Sigerson cup medal in 1971 with which college?

ANSWERS PAGE 229

GENERAL KNOWLEDGE

921 Who captained Kerry to the 2008 All-Ireland U-21 football title?

922 Who captained Galway to the 2007 All-Ireland U-21 hurling title?

923 Name the former All-Ireland winning hurling manager who managed UCD to Leinster club hurling finals in 2004 and 2005?

924 True or False? Kerry have never beaten Down in an All-Ireland football final at any level – minor, U-21 or senior?

925 An All-Ireland winning hurling captain from the last ten years managed a team in the 2008 Christy Ring Cup. Name him?

926 Who captained Tipperary to the 2007 All-Ireland minor hurling title?

927 True or False? The 2008 Fitzgibbon Cup final between WIT and LIT ended level after extra time and went to a second period of extra-time. If the sides had finished level again after that second period of extra-time, the match would have been decided on penalties.

928 Name the goalkeeper who played inter-county football in 2005 but who was only sub goalkeeper on his club team during their run in the provincial and All-Ireland club championships?

ANSWERS PAGE 229

929 Name the last father and son from Kilkenny to win All-Ireland senior hurling medals on the field of play (both won them in the last 25 years)?

930 Prior to 2008, name the only goalkeeper to receive a Christy Ring All-Star hurling award?

931 On how many occasions have a team which won a National Football League title (Division One) failed to secure an All-Star award – two, three or four?

932 Name the Dublin team which competed in the 2008 Nicky Rackard Cup?

933 London have failed to win a senior football championship game since which year – 1976, 1977 or 1978?

934 A member of Munster's Rugby Heineken Cup European successes in 2006 and 2008 won a county senior hurling medal with O'Loughlin Gaels in 2001. Name him?

935 Name the inter-county manager in the 2008 hurling championship who played as club goalkeeper in the 2008 Offlay club championahip?

936 An All-Ireland senior hurling semi-final was played in Armagh in the last 25 years. Name the year and the teams who contested the match?

ANSWERS PAGE 229

937 In 12 hurling championship matches between 1989-92, Tipperary had a full-forward line which scored 12-89 (with 27 of those points from frees). Name the three members of that full-forward line?

938 Name the multi-All-Ireland hurling medal winner with Kilkenny, and his son who won an All-Ireland medal with Cork in 1999?

939 In 13 hurling championship matches between 1990-92, Cork had a full-forward line which delivered 29-47 (1-5 from frees). Name the three members of that Cork full-forward line?

940 Prior to 2008, only three counties had failed to win an All-Star award in either code. Name those three counties?

KILKENNY GENERAL KNOWLEDGE

941 In which year did Christy Heffernan captain Kilkenny in an All-Ireland senior hurling final?

942 Name six of the seven Kilkenny clubs to have won Leinster club hurling titles?

943 In which year did Shane Doyle captain Kilkenny to an All-Ireland minor title?

944 How many All-Stars did Brian Cody win?

945 What year did Kilkenny win an All-Ireland minor title with a full-forward line of Adrian Ronan, Charlie Carter and DJ Carey?

946 Which county did Kilkenny beat in the 2008 national football league, to record their first win in competitive football in a decade?

947 After Noel Skehan, who holds the most All-Ireland senior medals in Kilkenny with eight?

948 In which year did Henry Shefflin and Michael Kavanagh play on a Kilkenny minor football team that was beaten by a point by a Laois team that subsequently went on to win the All-Ireland?

949 Name the Kilkenny hurler who made his championship debut in the 2000 All-Ireland final?

950 By which nickname is Martin Comerford commonly known?

951 Name the Kilkenny football manager in 2008?

ANSWERS PAGE 229

952 True or False? The Kilkenny team which won the 1957 All-Ireland title were record breakers in more ways than one because it was the only time in Kilkenny's All-Ireland winning history that junior clubs provided the majority of the starting 15.

953 Name the two Kilkenny brothers who between them won seven All-Ireland football medals with Dublin?

954 Name three of the four Kilkenny hurlers to win successive All-Stars (or more) in their thirties?

955 Name the only Kilkenny man to win All-Ireland senior hurling and football medals (although he did win his football medal with a different county)?

956 Apart from Paddy Buggy and Nickey Brennan, name the only other Kilkenny GAA President?

957 In the last ten years (prior to 2008) four sets of brothers have played in All-Ireland finals for Kilkenny. Name those four sets?

958 Name the only two players from Gowran to captain a Kilkenny team to an All-Ireland title (both were in the last 20 years)?

959 Denis Philpott, an All-Ireland minor winning selector with Kilkenny in 1991, won an All-Ireland minor football medal with which county in 1961?

960 The family record for All-Ireland senior hurling medals belongs to a Kilkenny family from Mooncoin who hold 18 among them. Name those three brothers?

ALL-IRELAND SENIOR HURLING FINALS FROM THE LAST 20 YEARS

961 Prior to 2008, name the only Munster county apart from Kerry not to contest an All-Ireland final in the last ten years?

962 Prior to 2008, in how many All-Ireland finals has Brian Cody managed Kilkenny?

963 Name the only player to captain his county in two All-Ireland finals in the last 20 years?

964 Name four of the five Clare players to play in the county's three All-Ireland final appearances between 1995-2002?

965 Name the Kilkenny forward to score goals in three of their six final appearances between 2000-07?

966 Only six Galway players started All-Ireland finals in 2001 and 2005. Name four of them?

967 Who captained Cork in the 2006 All-Ireland final?

968 Name the Limerick referee who took charge of three All-Ireland finals between 1999 and 2003?

969 True or False? Two teams from Leinster have contested an All-Ireland hurling final on one occasion (prior to 2008).

970 Who captained Offaly in the 1995 All-Ireland final?

ANSWERS PAGE 229

971 Name three of Cork's four goalscorers in the 1990 All-Ireland final against Galway?

972 Name the three Kilkenny players to win All-Ireland medals on the field of play in the 1990s and 2000s?

973 When Cork reached the 2006 All-Ireland final, they became only the second team in history to win 13 consecutive championship games. Which other team (prior to 2008) had surpassed that feat by winning 15 consecutive games (going 16 games unbeaten)?

974 Ciaran Barr, who captained Antrim in the 1989 All-Ireland final, later transferred to play hurling with which county?

975 Two sets of brothers have captained their county in All-Ireland finals over the last 20 years. Name them?

976 Name three of the five Tipperary players who played in All-Ireland finals in 1989, 1991 and 1997?

977 Name the only father and son to be involved an All-Ireland final as a referee and a player in the last 20 years?

978 Prior to 2008, there has only been one penalty scored in an All-Ireland final in the last 20 years. Name the goalscorer?

979 Name the only father and son to referee All-Ireland finals in the last 20 years?

980 In the last 20 years, five players have scored two goals in an All-Ireland final. Name four of them?

ANSWERS PAGE 229

FILL IN THE MISSING PARTS IN THE CLUB NAMES 2

981 Kilmacud

982 ...., Doora-Barefield

983 ...., Athenry

984 Kilruane-

985 ...., Rosslare

986 Duffry

987 ...., Carrick-on-Shannon

988 ...., Dungiven (hurling)

989 ...., Dungiven (football)

990 Ballymun

991 Moycarkey-

992 ...., Letterkenny

993 Cashel King

994 Lough Lene

995 ...., Myshall

996 Upperchurch-

997 Mountbellew/

998 Conahy

999 Carnew

1000 Mullaghbawn

ANSWERS PAGE 230

LAOIS GENERAL KNOWLEDGE

1001 Who captained Portlaoise in the 2005 All-Ireland club final?

1002 In which year did Camross last win the Leinster club hurling championship?

1003 Who managed Laois to the 1996 All-Ireland minor football title?

1004 Name the only Laois hurler in the top 20 All-time senior hurling championship scorers?

1005 Name the three Laois clubs who have contested Leinster club football finals?

1006 Name the two Tipperary men who managed the Laois hurlers (in two separate terms) between 2003-06?

1007 Who managed the Laois senior football team before Mick O'Dwyer took over in 2003?

1008 Name the three brothers who have played senior hurling and football for Laois in the last 15 years?

1009 Name the only GAA President from Laois?

1010 Castletown lost three Leinster club hurling finals to Birr between 1997 and 2001 but in which of those three finals did they take Birr to a replay?

ANSWERS PAGE 230

1011 In which year did Colm Begley return from playing with Brisbane Lions in the AFL and line out with Stradbally in a county senior football final?

1012 Who captained Laois to their first National League football title in 1986?

1013 The family record for Railway Cup medals (18) is held by which Laois family?

1014 Who captained Laois to the 1997 All-Ireland minor title?

1015 Name the Laois player who scored the winning goal against Dublin with the last puck of the game in the 2001 Leinster hurling quarter-final?

1016 Name the goalkeeper who captained Laois to the 2002 National League Division Two hurling title?

1017 Name the Laois goalkeeper who scored a penalty in the 1992 Leinster quarter-final against Meath, which effectively knocked the Leinster champions out of the competition?

1018 Name the Laois player who captained St Kieran's, Kilkenny to the 2004 All-Ireland Colleges title?

1019 Name the only Laois player to be named on the GAA's hurling Centenary team, comprising players who had never won an All-Ireland senior medal?

1020 Name the Laois man who refereed five All-Ireland football finals in a row between 1915-19?

ANSWERS PAGE 230

GAA POLITICIANS

1021 Name the football manager who was voted into the Dáil during the 2007 championship season?

1022 Name the politician who captained Kerry to the 1981 All-Ireland title?

1023 Name the former Wexford hurling manager who was elected to the Dáil in 2002, while he was still manager?

1024 The late politician Liam Lawlor played hurling with which county?

1025 Two former All-Ireland winning football captains from the last 15 years ran for election in 2007. Name them?

1026 Name the player who went from winning an All-Ireland medal with Cavan in 1947 to Tánaiste 33 years later?

1027 True or False? Jack Lynch first ran for the Dáil in 1948, just three years after he had become the first and only player in history to win five All-Ireland medals in a row.

1028 Name the All-Ireland football three-in-a-row winner with Galway in the 1960s who was elected to the Dáil?

1029 Former TD Hugh Gibbons won an All-Ireland with which county in the 1940s?

ANSWERS PAGE 230

1030 Name the former Mayo All-Ireland double winning captain who led the county to All-Ireland titles in 1950 and 1951 and was subsequently elected a TD?

1031 He was a politician who won All-Ireland medals in 1903 and 1904 and the county grounds in Tralee are named after him. Name him?

1032 He won an All-Ireland with Dublin in 1963 and holds the unique distinction of having won Railway Cup medals on the same day before being voted into the Dáil. Name him?

1033 Sean Brosnan won All-Irelands in 1937, 1940 and 1941 with which county before being elected a TD?

1034 Tom O'Reilly from Cavan who won All-Ireland medals in 1933, 1935 and 1947 and who was later elected to the Dáil, was more commonly known by which nickname?

1035 Name the only father and son to win All-Ireland medals and be elected TDs?

1036 The father of Fine Gael Party leader Enda Kenny won an All-Ireland medal with Mayo in 1936. Name him?

1037 Name the man who captained Kerry to an All-Ireland title in 1940 and who secured a Labour seat in Tralee for almost 40 years?

ANSWERS PAGE 230

1038 In the last ten years, one manager who managed a team in an All-Ireland hurling final made it to the last count as a Fianna Fáil candidate in the 1992 poll before being narrowly defeated. Name him?

1039 Name the former Dublin county board chairman and current politician who refereed the 1986 All-Ireland hurling final?

1040 He won a Leinster football medal with Wexford in 1945, was Labour leader in the 1960s and Tánaiste in the early 1970s. Name him?

ODD ONE OUT

1041 Crossmolina, Castlebar Mitchells, Ballina Stephenites.

1042 Waterford IT, Limerick IT, Cork IT.

1043 Henry Shefflin, Martin Comerford, James 'Cha' Fitzpatrick.

1044 O'Moore Park, Markievicz Park, O'Connor Park.

1045 Dungiven, Ballinderry, Bellaghy.

1046 Nickey Brennan, Paddy Buggy, Con Murphy.

1047 Clarecastle, Patrickswell, Sixmilebridge.

1048 IT Tralee, Sligo IT, DIT.

1049 Cyril Farrell, Noel Lane, John McIntrye.

1050 David Brady, James Nallen, Ciaran McDonald.

1051 Paul Hearty, Pat Mullaney, Alan Quirke.

1052 Eugene McGee, Billy Morgan, John Maughan.

1053 Tommy Dowd, Graham Geraghty, Trevor Giles.

1054 O'Keeffe Cup, O'Duffy Cup, Nestor Cup.

1055 Dr Crokes, Austin Stacks, An Ghaeltacht.

1056 Ben O'Connor, Diarmuid O'Sullivan, Seán Óg Ó hAilpín.

1057 Seán Ó Síocháin, Dr Mick Loftus, Liam Mulvihill.

1058 Kilruane McDonagh's, Toomevara, Roscrea.

1059 Joe Lennon, James McCartan and Paddy Doherty.

1060 North Monastery, Thurles CBS, Limerick CBS.

ANSWERS PAGE 230

LEITRIM GENERAL KNOWLEDGE

1061 Who managed Leitrim to the 2000 Connacht final?

1062 Which county defeated Leitrim in the 2006 Tommy Murphy Cup final?

1063 Name the four Leitrim clubs to contest Connacht club football finals?

1064 Who managed Leitrim to the All-Ireland B title in 1990?

1065 Name the only Leitrim player selected on the GAA's Centenary Football Team, comprising players who never won an All-Ireland senior medal?

1066 Name the Leitrim senior football panellist in 2007, who played against Leitrim in the championship for New York in 2008?

1067 In which year did Mickey Quinn win a first All-Star for Leitrim?

1068 Who succeeded John O'Mahony as Leitrim manager in 1997?

1069 Who did Leitrim defeat to record their first ever All-Ireland Intermediate Ladies' football title in 2007?

1070 Name the 34-year-old veteran who scored 0-8 in the above match?

ANSWERS PAGE 231

1071 Name the goalkeeper who captained Leitrim in the 2000 Connacht senior final?

1072 In which year did Declan Darcy play his last championship match for Leitrim before joining Dublin?

1073 Name the two Leitrim players to have played International Rules Football?

1074 Which club holds the most county senior hurling titles?

1075 Who captained the first Leitrim team to win a Connacht senior football title in 1927 and was present in 1994 to help Declan Darcy lift the trophy for the second time?

1076 What famous scalp did Leitrim take in the first NFL match of 1990-91 season?

1077 Name the last Leitrim player to win an Interprovincial medal (formerly Railway Cup) on the field of play?

1078 Kerry beat Leitrim in the 1927 All-Ireland semi-final in which Connacht town?

1079 In the 1995 Connacht semi-final, when Leitrim relinquished their Connacht title, Galway won the game with an injury-time free scored by which player?

1080 Name the three clubs that were part of the Sheemore Gaels (amalgamation) that won its only county senior football title in 1974?

ANSWERS PAGE 231

MATCH THE FOOTBALLER TO HIS CLUB

1081 Jason Sherlock (Dublin)

1082 Paul Galvin (Kerry)

1083 Graham Canty (Cork)

1084 Declan Meehan (Galway)

1085 Paul Hearty (Armagh)

1086 Joe Higgins (Laois)

1087 Conor Gormley (Tyrone)

1088 Martin Flanagan (Westmeath)

1089 Niall McNamee (Offaly)

1090 Ronan McGarrity (Mayo)

1091 Dermot Earley (Kildare)

1092 Thomas Freeman (Monaghan)

1093 Liam Doyle (Down)

1094 Ryan McCluskey (Fermanagh)

1095 Kevin Cassidy (Donegal)

1096 Frankie Dolan (Roscommon)

1097 Tommy Gill (Wicklow)

1098 Fergal Doherty (Derry)

1099 Redmond Barry (Wexford)

1100 Seanie Johnston (Cavan)

ANSWERS PAGE 231

FOOTBALL GENERAL KNOWLEDGE

1101 Name the Derry player who won six Railway Cup medals in a row on the field of play between 1989 and 1995 (there was no competition in 1990)?

1102 Name the referee who officiated for the four Dublin-Meath games in 1991?

1103 Armagh's Kieran McGeeney played in an All-Ireland club football final in 2000 with which club?

1104 Name the current inter-county football manager who was part of Kevin Heffernan's International Rules backroom team in 1986?

1105 Name the Kerry player who captained the county in two National League finals in the last five years?

1106 Which county won the 2008 National League Division 3 title after extra-time?

1107 Name the father and sons who were involved with different Connacht and Leinster counties in the 2008 football championship?

1108 Name the Fermanagh footballer who played in the 2008 Ulster final and who also lined out with St Gall's in the 2006 All-Ireland club final?

1109 Name the two clubs in Arles in Laois?

1110 In which year did Mickey Harte play in an Ulster final with Tyrone?

1111 The only International Rules Tests played outside Croke Park were in which two venues?

1112 Prior to 2008, name the three brothers who won Ulster titles with Armagh in the previous ten years on the field of play?

1113 Who refereed the infamous 1983 All-Ireland football final between Dublin and Galway, when four players were sent off?

1114 Name the Kerryman who managed Munster to the 2007 Interprovincial final?

1115 Which county overhauled an eight-point deficit in the last seven minutes to draw the 2007 All-Ireland minor semi-final with Derry?

1116 Name the Galway goalkeeper who became the first keeper to keep clean sheets in three successive All-Ireland finals?

1117 Who were the only club to contest a provincial club final in the last ten years, despite not having won their own county senior title?

1118 Name the only goalkeeper to keep clean sheets in 60, 70 and 80-minute All-Ireland finals?

1119 Which football manager had his son as part of his backroom team during the 2007 championship?

1120 Pat Spillane was only held scoreless in seven of his 56 championship games with Kerry but name the player who kept him scoreless in three of those seven matches?

ANSWERS PAGE 231

LIMERICK GENERAL KNOWLEDGE

1121 Who managed Limerick to their three All-Ireland U-21 hurling titles between 2000-02?

1122 Which county did Limerick defeat in the 2002 National football league to record a win against that opposition for the first time in nearly 100 years?

1123 Who captained Limerick in the 2007 Munster hurling final?

1124 Which county defeated Limerick in the 2003 Division Two Football National League final?

1125 Who captained Limerick to the 2000 All-Ireland U-21 hurling title?

1126 Name the three Limerick clubs to contest All-Ireland club hurling finals?

1127 Name the only Limerick player to play league hurling and football in 2008?

1128 Name the two hurling goalkeepers that Limerick used during their two games in the 2004 championship?

1129 Name the only Limerick player to win an Interprovincial (formerly Railway Cup) football medal with Munster on the field of play in the last 25 years?

1130 Who captained Limerick to the 1992 National hurling League title?

ANSWERS PAGE 231

1131 In which year did University of Limerick and Limerick IT contest the Fitzgibbon Cup final?

1132 Name the former Tipperary football manager who coached Ballylanders to the 2007 county football title?

1133 In which year did Joe McKenna play his last game for the Limerick hurlers – 1983, 1984 or 1985?

1134 Limerick hurler Mike O'Brien is commonly known by which nickname?

1135 There are three Limerick hurlers in the top 20 all-time senior hurling championship scorers (prior to 2008). Name two of them?

1136 Who managed Limerick to the 1991 Munster football final?

1137 Who captained Limerick to their first All-Ireland U-21 hurling title in 1987?

1138 Who managed the Limerick footballers before Liam Kearns took over in 1999?

1139 Only three hurlers have played in Interprovincial finals in three different decades. One is a Limerick man. Name him?

1140 Name the Limerick footballer who played International Rules in 1990?

ANSWERS PAGE 231

CROKE PARK – A HISTORY

1141 In 1913, the GAA purchased Jones' Road (now Croke Park) from which individual?

1142 In which year did 'Bloody Sunday' take place in Croke Park – 1919, 1920 or 1921?

1143 On how many occasions was the Tailteann games held in Croke Park between 1924-32?

1144 The most unusual event ever held in Croke Park took place for one week in August 1924. It involved horses. What was it?

1145 The Hogan Stand was officially opened in 1926 in honour of Michael Hogan who was killed during Bloody Sunday. With which county was Hogan playing when he was shot?

1146 The Cusack Stand was officially opened in which year – 1938, 1939 or 1940?

1147 The Canal End Terrace opened in which year – 1950, 1951 or 1952?

1148 The small stand at the northwest corner of the ground was opened in 1952. After which leading figure in the Irish Republican Brotherhood and a founding member and secretary of the Land League was the stand named?

1149 The New Hogan Stand was officially opened in the 75th year of the GAA. Which year?

ANSWERS PAGE 231

1150 A record crowd of 90,556 turned up at Croke Park for the 1961 All-Ireland football final between which two counties?

1151 Teilifís Éireann broadcast its first live television game from Croke Park in which year – 1962, 1963 or 1964?

1152 Events commemorating the fiftieth anniversary of which historic Irish event were held in Croke Park in 1966?

1153 The Willwood Tailteann Games were held in Croke Park in which year – 1972, 1973 or 1974?

1154 The first series of International Rules Games were held in Croke Park in which year during the 1980s?

1155 Which famous Irish band played a sell-out concert in Croke Park in 1985?

1156 Hill 16 was reconstructed and reopened in which year during the 1980s?

1157 Demolition of the Cusack Stand, as part of the redevelopment of Croke Park, began in which year?

1158 In which year did demolition of the Hogan Stand begin?

1159 The opening and closing ceremonies of which famous international event was staged at Croke Park in 2003?

1160 Which two counties played the first game under lights in Croke Park in 2007?

ANSWERS PAGE 231

UNLUCKY AND UNFORTUNATE INCIDENTS

1161 Name the Westmeath player who had a chance from a 20-metre free to win the game against Meath (and secure Westmeath's first championship win against Meath) in the 2003 Leinster championship but who kicked the ball wide?

1162 The decisive goal in the 2002 Munster hurling semi-final between Cork and Waterford came from a long delivery that bounced and deceived Donal Óg Cusack. Name the goalscorer?

1163 In the 1995 All-Ireland hurling final, Clare's Davy Fitzgerald tried to control a shot on his hurley but the ball just slipped behind the line. Name the Offaly goalscorer?

1164 With just a couple of minutes remaining in the 1994 Leinster football final between Dublin and Meath, a long free from Charlie Redmond was dropped into the net by the goalkeeper and Meath were beaten by one point. It was the unfortunate goalkeeper's last championship game after a distinguished career. Name him?

1165 Name the Dublin forward who hit the post with a last-second free in the 2002 All-Ireland semi-final, which Armagh won by a point?

1166 In the 1996 All-Ireland football semi-final between Kerry and Mayo, Sean Burke launched a long ball upfield but the Mayo keeper jumped to gather it into his midriff only to let it past him and into the net. He later claimed that he had been watching a replay of James Nallen's goal on the big screen. Name the goalkeeper?

ANSWERS PAGE 232

1167 In the dying minutes of the 1984 Munster hurling semi-final, Limerick were leading by two points when a long-range sideline slipped through the fingers of goalkeeper Tommy Quaid. Cork went on to win the All-Ireland but who scored that goal?

1168 Name the Galway goalkeeper who conceded two goals from long-range strikes in the 1979 All-Ireland hurling final against Kilkenny?

1169 In the 1986 All-Ireland football semi-final between Kerry and Meath, Ogie Moran drilled a high ball towards the square. Meath full-back Mick Lyons, corner-back Joe Cassells and goalkeeper Mickey McQuillan all went for the ball but were soon all sprawling on the ground while a Kerry forward gathered the ball and clipped it into an empty net. Name that Kerry goalscorer?

1170 In the 1938 All-Ireland football final, the referee blew for a free to Kerry with two minutes remaining but the team in the lead thought that he had blown the final whistle and the crowd invaded the pitch. Nine of the Kerry players left the pitch and some had even returned to the Central Hotel to change there. Some of the subs came on while the injured Joe Keohane, who was sitting innocently in the stands in a suit, was also pressed into action. Name the county though, who won that game?

1171 In the 2001 All-Ireland hurling final, the Galway goalkeeper Michael Crimmins came out to deal with a low kicked shot but the ball ran under his legs and into the net. Name the Tipperary goalscorer?

1172 After Kerry won their 19th All-Ireland football title in 1959, the Kerry captain forgot to bring the Sam Maguire with him from the dressing room. Name the Kerry captain?

1173 In the 1993 All-Ireland hurling semi-final between Galway and Tipperary, Galway were trailing by 0-2 to 0-0 after six minutes and had made little headway in attack when a harmless effort for a point bounced in front of Ken Hogan, hit him on the shoulder and trickled into the net. Hogan went on to have a fine game but Tipp lost by two points and it was his last championship match. Name the Galway goalscorer?

1174 With the last play of the 2005 Division Two National League final between Monaghan and Meath, a Paul Finlay free dropped on the goal-line and a Meath player who tried to punch the ball over the bar, fisted it into his own net for the winning score. Name the unfortunate Meath player?

1175 In the 1993 All-Ireland hurling final, a midfield delivery squirmed behind Kilkenny goalkeeper Michael Walsh. Although Walsh got back to hook the ball clear, the sliotar had just crossed the line. Name the Galway goalscorer?

1176 Name the Dublin midfielder who missed a close-in free which would have won the 2000 (drawn) Leinster football final against Kildare?

1177 Name the Laois defender who scored an unfortunate own goal against Offaly in the 1996 Leinster hurling semi-final, after slipping near the goal-line as he was about to clear?

ANSWERS PAGE 232

1178 The decisive score in the 1992 National League football final came from an Anthony Tohill '45 that went all the way to the net, but name the Tyrone midfielder who missed the catch just in front of goalkeeper Finbar McConnell?

1179 Name the unfortunate Limerick defender who scored an own goal in the 1984 Munster hurling semi-final against Cork?

1180 With the sides level in the dying minutes of the 2005 Leinster club hurling final, the UCD goalkeeper dropped a long ball, which hit the post and a goal was subsequently scored. Immediately afterwards, the 'keeper was picked off for a short puckout which resulted in a point. That goalkeeper was a Laois defender. Name him?

LONGFORD GENERAL KNOWLEDGE

1181 From which club did former GAA Ard Stiúrthóir, Liam Mulvihill, hail?

1182 Longford won their only Leinster senior football title in 1968 but which county defeated them in that year's All-Ireland semi-final?

1183 Who scored the winning point for Longford in injury-time of their classic Round 3 qualifier game with Derry in 2006?

1184 Which county defeated Longford in the 2006 Leinster U-21 football final?

1185 Who did Longford defeat in the first round of the 2007 Leinster championship?

1186 Name the Longford official who lost the GAA Presidential race to Sean McCague in 1999?

1187 Which Dublin club did Brian Kavanagh transfer to in 2008?

1188 Name the Longford player who was top scorer in the Nicky Rackard Cup in 2005 with a tally of 3-30?

1189 Longford never won an All-Ireland B football title but how many finals did they contest – two, three or four?

1190 Who captained the Longford minor footballers to the 2002 Leinster minor title?

ANSWERS PAGE 232

1191 How many All-Ireland Colleges titles have St Mel's, Longford won?

1192 From which club did Eugene McGee hail?

1193 Name the former All-Ireland winning manager to have managed Longford in the last 20 years?

1194 True or False? Longford are the only county in the country to have never produced a provincial club finalist (in either hurling or football)?

1195 Name the three brothers who played with Longford in the 2001 football championship?

1196 Who managed Longford to the O'Byrne Cup title in 2000?

1197 Who managed the Longford hurlers in 2008?

1198 Name the inter-county manager from the 2008 football championship who managed Longford to the 1991 All-Ireland B football final against Clare?

1199 Name the three Longford players to have represented Ireland at International Rules level?

1200 In the 1997 Leinster Colleges final, the St Mel's coach Declan Rowley was involved in a highly controversial incident when he went to talk to one of his players and an opposing player pushed the St Mel's player in the back, causing a clash of heads and leaving Rowley with a black eye and swollen face. Which college was that opposing player from?

ANSWERS PAGE 232.

GENERAL KNOWLEDGE

1201 Which college hosted the 2008 Sigerson Cup?

1202 Which college hosted the 2008 Fitzgibbon Cup?

1203 True or False? Cork and Tipperary never met in the Munster hurling championship between 1993 and 1999.

1204 Who captained Ireland's first International Rules team against Australia in 1984?

1205 How long is an inter-county U-21 championship game, 60 or 70 minutes?

1206 In the last 25 years, three counties have managed to appear in minor hurling and football finals in the same season. Name those three counties?

1207 Name the three candidates who ran for the GAA Presidential election in 2008?

1208 Name the three counties in Leinster that Luke Dempsey has managed in the last ten years?

1209 Name the Wexford man who captained the county to the 1956 All-Ireland title and who sadly passed away in 2008?

1210 Name the Tipperary footballer who won an All-Ireland club medal with St Vincent's in 2008?

ANSWERS PAGE 232

1211 True or False? Waterford were beaten in the first round of the Munster championship for five consecutive seasons in the 1990s.

1212 Name the former Armagh selector who went to Kildare as part of Kieran McGeeney's backroom team?

1213 Name the former Kilkenny hurler who played championship hurling with Tipperary in 2003?

1214 Name the former Kilkenny and Offaly manager who was appointed Dublin Director of Hurling in 2003?

1215 Apart from Alan Kerins, name the only other player to play in an All-Ireland hurling and football quarter-final in the last ten years (prior to 2008)?

1216 Who were the first Ulster club to reach an All-Ireland club hurling final?

1217 Name the only county to contest a Tommy Murphy Cup final and to win a provincial title?

1218 Name the four Antrim clubs to contest All-Ireland club hurling finals?

1219 Name the only father and son to win a Provincial club hurling medal in the last 20 years?

1220 Name the two brothers who managed teams in the 2008 Leinster hurling championship?

MANAGERIAL ROLL CALL 2

1221 Who managed Derry to the 2008 National League title?

1222 Who managed Tipperary to the 2008 National League hurling title?

1223 Name the former Derry football All-Star who managed the Derry senior hurlers in 2008?

1224 Name the only two hurling managers to have managed counties in Munster and Leinster over the last ten years?

1225 Who managed Armagh in the 2008 Ulster senior football final?

1226 Who managed Portumna to the 2008 All-Ireland club title?

1227 How many managers did Roscommon have in the football championship between 2004 and 2008 – three, four or five?

1228 In the last 15 years, two Derry managers have had sons on the Derry team while they were manager. Name both managers and both sons?

1229 Who managed Cork to the 2008 Munster senior football final?

1230 Name the priest, who managed Clare to successive hurling league titles in 1977 and 1978, and who was a selector with Clare between 2004-06?

1231 The former Offaly hurler, Michael Duignan, managed which Leinster county in the 2002 and 2003 Leinster championship?

ANSWERS PAGE 232

1232 Name the only manager to have managed two different counties in the Munster hurling championship over the last ten years?

1233 Name the only manager to manage a team in an All-Ireland club final and an inter-county team in an All-Ireland senior football final in the same season?

1234 Which hurling county has changed their hurling manager 14 times in the last 20 years?

1235 Which county did Barney Rock manage in the Leinster football championship over the last 15 years?

1236 A manager from the 2008 hurling championship coached Cashel King Cormacs to the 1991 Munster club hurling title. Name him?

1237 Name the manager who managed in the 2008 football championship and who was also player-manager in the 1974 All-Ireland football final?

1238 Name the only manager to have managed two different counties in the Munster football championship over the last 20 years?

1239 Name the former Galway double All-Ireland winner from 1987-88 who was player-manager with the Kinvara side that reached the 2007 Galway county hurling final?

1240 Name the only hurling manager to have managed/coached teams to provincial hurling success in the 1970s, 1980s and 2000s?

LOUTH GENERAL KNOWLEDGE

1241 In which town is Newtown Blues?

1242 Which club did former Down All-Ireland winning manager Pete McGrath coach to a county final in the last five years?

1243 With which two clubs does Aaron Hoey play hurling and football?

1244 In which year did Louth win the All-Ireland B Football title?

1245 Which county did Louth defeat after a replay to win the 2006 National League Division Two football title?

1246 Name the father and son who were part of the Louth hurling squad who reached the 2006 Nicky Rackard Cup final?

1247 In which year did Dundalk Colleges win the Leinster Colleges football title – 2001, 2002 or 2003?

1248 Name the only two Louth clubs to contest a Leinster club football final?

1249 Who managed Louth to the 2000 Division Two National League football title?

1250 Name the only Louth player to be selected on the GAA's Centenary football team, comprising players who never won an All-Ireland senior medal?

1251 Name the only Louth player nominated for a football All-Star in the last ten years?

ANSWERS PAGE 232

1252 Paul Dunne became the first Louthman to win the All-Ireland Poc Fada title. He won the award in which year – 2001, 2002 or 2003?

1253 Former Louth player Stefan White also played with which other county?

1254 When Louth won their first All-Ireland title in 1910, they didn't play an All-Ireland final because they received a walkover from which county?

1255 Who scored Louth's only goal in the 1957 All-Ireland football final?

1256 Name the former Louth player who won two All-Ireland club football titles with Crossmaglen Rangers?

1257 True or False? Dermot O'Brien, the last man to captain Louth to an All-Ireland title in 1957, hosted his own TV show on RTE, while also hosting a TV show in the US.

1258 Which Louth club played in the first All-Ireland football final in 1887?

1259 Although Louth had a player nominated for an All-Star in 2007, their previous All-Star nominee was in 1981. He was a goalkeeper. Name him?

1260 Which new landmark has been recently incorporated into the Louth county crest with the St Brigid's crest?

MAJOR GAA GROUNDS

1261 The first Munster hurling final staged in the Sportsfield in Thurles was held in 1914 between Cork and Clare. The referee for that game had captained Tipperary to All-Ireland hurling titles in 1906 and 1908 and when the Sportsfield was later redeveloped, it was renamed after that individual. Name him?

1262 The modern Páirc Uí Chaoimh was first opened in which year – 1976, 1977 or 1978?

1263 Which county grounds closed in 2007 for redevelopment work and reopened for a big Ulster football championship quarter-final in 2008?

1264 Apart from Croke Park, name the only GAA ground to stage an International Rules game in the last ten years?

1265 The Kerry county ground in Killarney is named after which famous Kerry footballer?

1266 What is the name of the Waterford county ground in Waterford City?

1267 The Roscommon county ground in Roscommon town is named after which former Irish president?

1268 Prior to 2008, name the only county ground to sell its name?

1269 What is the name of the GAA grounds in Navan?

1270 Which GAA club are based at the Mayo county ground, McHale Park?

1271 The 2007 All-Ireland club football final replay was played at which ground?

1272 Where is the only major GAA venue which has synthetic grass as a pitch surface?

1273 Although O'Connor Park in Tullamore is the main county grounds in Offaly, what is the name of the GAA grounds in Birr?

1274 Páirc Esler in Newry is still more commonly known by which name?

1275 One of the first grounds owned by the GAA was in Belfast, which was opened in 1927. Name it?

1276 The GAA ground, Páirc Uí Rinn, was a previously well-established soccer ground under which name?

1277 The stadium in St Tiernach's Park in Clones was completely modernised, with uncovered seating replacing the famous "hill", a stand erected and a new pitch laid in time for which year's Ulster football final over the last 15 years?

1278 The Mackey Stand in Limerick's Gaelic Grounds was officially opened on the day of which Munster hurling final in the last 20 years?

1279 What is the name of the main Stand in Brewster Park, Enniskillen?

1280 What is the proper name of Tuam Stadium?

ANSWERS PAGE 233

INDIVIDUAL TOP SCORERS IN ALL-IRELAND HURLING FINALS OVER THE LAST 35 YEARS

1281 Who was top scorer in the 2007 All-Ireland final with 1-5?

1282 Name the Kilkenny player who was top scorer in the 2006 All-Ireland final?

1283 In which year's All-Ireland final did DJ Carey finish top scorer with 2-4?

1284 The top scorer in the 2005 All-Ireland final scored 1-7. Name him?

1285 Name the Kilkenny forward who was top scorer in the 2003 All-Ireland final with 1-4 (all from play)?

1286 Name the Clare player who finished top scorer in the 1997 final with 0-7?

1287 Prior to 2008, on how many occasions was Henry Shefflin top scorer in an All-Ireland final – two, three or four?

1288 Who was the top scorer in the 1998 All-Ireland final with 1-6?

1289 Name the Kilkenny midfielder who finished top scorer in the 1987 All-Ireland final, even though he was on the losing side?

1290 He won an All-Ireland minor medal in 1991 and was top scorer in an All-Ireland senior final just two years later. Name him?

ANSWERS PAGE 233

1291 DJ Carey was top scorer in an All-Ireland final on how many occasions – one, two or three?

1292 Name the two Cork players who were joint-top scorers in the 1986 All-Ireland final with a combined total of 3-5?

1293 Name the Galway player who finished top scorer with 1-6 but was on the losing side in the 1985 All-Ireland final against Offaly?

1294 Name the Limerick player who scored 2-7 in the 1980 All-Ireland final and still finished on the losing side?

1295 In which year's All-Ireland final did Christy Heffernan finish as top scorer with 2-3?

1296 Name the Cork player who hit 0-10 in the 1976 All-Ireland final?

1297 Name the Limerick midfielder who hit 0-10 in the 1973 All-Ireland final?

1298 Name the two Cork players who finished joint-top scorers in the 1984 Centenary All-Ireland hurling final with a combined total of 2-8?

1299 Prior to 2008, four players have managed to hit ten scores or more in an All-Ireland final. Name three of them?

1300 Prior to 2008, three players from the losing All-Ireland final team have finished top scorer in All-Ireland finals in the last 20 years. Name them?

ANSWERS PAGE 233

MAYO GENERAL KNOWLEDGE

1301 David Clarke played in goal for the 2006 All-Ireland final but who was the goalkeeper for the Connacht title success that year?

1302 Name the joint-managers who led Mayo to their first All-Ireland ladies' football title in 1999?

1303 Who scored Mayo's opening goal in the 2004 All-Ireland final after only four minutes?

1304 Name the player who played in Connacht club hurling and football finals in 2007 with Ballina Stephenites and James Stephen's?

1305 Name the Mayo player who played in the 1996 and 1997 All-Ireland senior finals as a forward and who won a Connacht club title in 2001 as a goalkeeper?

1306 Name the two former Mayo footballers who won an All-Ireland club football title with Salthill-Knocknacarra in 2006?

1307 How many Connacht club hurling finals have Tooreen contested – five, ten or fifteen?

1308 Name the 42-year-old player who featured for Mayo in the drawn 1985 All-Ireland semi-final against Dublin?

1309 Name the two Mayo players selected on the GAA's Centenary Football Team, comprising players who never won an All-Ireland senior medal?

ANSWERS PAGE 233

1310 Who scored Mayo's only goal in 1996 replayed All-Ireland final against Meath?

1311 How many Connacht titles did Martin Carney win with Mayo after he transferred from Donegal?

1312 In which year did Mayo lose to Kerry after extra-time in the Division Two National Hurling League semi-final (it was in the last five years)?

1313 Name the Mayo forward who scored a classic goal in the 1985 drawn All-Ireland semi-final against Dublin?

1314 In which year did John O'Mahony manage Mayo to an All-Ireland U-21 title?

1315 Apart from Tooreen and James Stephens, name the only other Mayo club to contest a Connacht club hurling final?

1316 Who captained Mayo to their first All-Ireland ladies' football title in 1999?

1317 Name the former manager who won two Division One National Hurling League titles and who managed the Mayo hurlers for one season in 2002?

1318 Name two of the three Mayo players who were part of the Connacht hurling squad that contested the 2007 Interprovincial final?

1319 Name the Mayo player who hit the equalising point against Dublin in the drawn All-Ireland semi-final in 1985?

1320 When Connacht won successive Railway Cup hurling titles in 1982 and 1983, the goalkeeper was a Mayo man. Name him?

ALL-IRELAND FOOTBALL FINALS FROM THE LAST 20 YEARS

1321 Who scored Cork's only goal in the 2007 All-Ireland football final?

1322 How many goals did Kieran Donaghy score in the 2006 and 2007 All-Ireland finals?

1323 Prior to 2008, how many teams had won the All-Ireland title having come through the qualifiers (and name them)?

1324 Name the player who captained his county to an All-Ireland title, 14 years after he had played in an All-Ireland hurling semi-final?

1325 Prior to 2008, name the player who missed penalties in two All-Ireland finals in the last 20 years?

1326 In the 1990s, two All-Ireland finals failed to produce a goal. Which finals?

1327 Who scored the only goal in the 1996 drawn All-Ireland final between Meath and Mayo?

1328 Prior to 2008, who was the last player to be sent off in an All-Ireland football final?

1329 Name the two Tyrone players to play in All-Ireland finals in 1995 and 2005?

1330 Name the last player to start All-Ireland hurling and football finals in the same year?

1331 Who scored Derry's only goal in the 1993 All-Ireland final?

1332 Joe Cassells captained Meath in the 1988 replayed All-Ireland final but who captained Meath in the drawn game?

1333 In the last 20 years, only two defenders have scored goals in All-Ireland finals. Name them?

1334 Prior to 2008, three goalkeepers have saved penalties in All-Ireland finals in the last 20 years. Name them?

1335 Four players have captained their county in successive All-Ireland finals in the last 20 years. Name them?

1336 Who scored the only goal in the 1989 All-Ireland final between Cork and Mayo?

1337 Name the only two Kerry players to win five All-Ireland medals on the field of play in the last two decades (prior to 2008)?

1338 Name the player sent off in the 1990 All-Ireland final between Meath and Cork?

1339 Two captains have scored goals in All-Ireland finals over the last 20 years. Name them?

1340 In the last 15 years, two players have captained their county to an All-Ireland final in their debut season. Name them?

ANSWERS PAGE 233

COUNTY ANTHEMS AND SONGS

eg Clare – My lovely Rose of Clare

1341 Antrim

1342 Armagh

1343 Cork

1344 Donegal

1345 Down

1346 Dublin

1347 Galway

1348 Kerry

1349 Kildare

1350 Kilkenny

1351 Laois

1352 Leitrim

1353 Limerick

1354 Mayo

1355 Meath

1356 Offaly

1357 Tipperary

1358 Tyrone

1359 Wexford

1360 Wicklow

ANSWERS PAGE 233

MEATH GENERAL KNOWLEDGE

1361 Graham Geraghty now plays with Clan na Gael but with which club did he originally play?

1362 Name the former Meath hurler who captained London to the 2006 Nicky Rackard Cup title?

1363 How many games did Meath play during the 1991 football championship?

1364 Name the Meath player sent off in the 2001 All-Ireland senior football final against Galway?

1365 Name the former Tipperary hurler who played with Meath in the 2007 Christy Ring Cup?

1366 Who did Meath beat in the 1993 All-Ireland U-21 football final to record their first All-Ireland success in that grade?

1367 Name the Meath hurler who hit 0-15 against Kildare in the first round of the 2001 Leinster hurling championship?

1368 Name the three members of the Meath All-Ireland winning team from 1996 who were suspended for the 1997 Leinster final against Offaly?

1369 Who was Meath's first football All-Star?

1370 In which year did Meath last play in Division One of the National Hurling League – 2001, 2002 or 2003?

ANSWERS PAGE 234

1371 How many All-Ireland Colleges football titles did St Pat's Navan win between 2000- 06 – one, two or three?

1372 Who were the last team to beat Meath with Sean Boylan as manager?

1373 Name four of the five Meath clubs to contest Leinster club football finals?

1374 Name the two Meath players who have won four All-Stars?

1375 Along with St Pat's Navan, name the only other Meath College to win an All-Ireland Colleges football title?

1376 Who was the last Meath hurler to win an Interprovincial (formerly Railway Cup) medal with Leinster as a starter (it was in the last 15 years)?

1377 Name the Meath All-Ireland medal winner from 1987 and 1988 who was sent off in the 1992 Leinster quarter-final against Laois and who retired that evening?

1378 Who captained Meath to the 1992 All-Ireland minor title?

1379 When Meath defeated Laois in the 2002 Leinster hurling championship, name the player who sensationally hit a last-gasp winning goal?

1380 Who captained Meath to the 1994 National Football League title?

ANSWERS PAGE 234

SOME OF HURLING'S GREAT PLAYERS FROM THE LAST 30 YEARS

1381 How many All-Ireland club medals did Kilkenny's Joe Hennessy win with James Stephens?

1382 Name the Offaly centre-back who got man of the match in the 1981 All-Ireland final?

1383 Cork's Ger Cunningham was voted Texaco Hurler of the Year in which season?

1384 Joe Cooney hit 1-22 in how many final appearances for Galway?

1385 Brian Lohan played in an All-Ireland club hurling final for Wolfe Tones in which season?

1386 With which club did Joe McKenna play in Limerick?

1387 In which year did Liam Dunne play his last championship match for Wexford?

1388 The player with the greatest average in All-Ireland finals (0-8) is from Tipperary. Name him?

1389 Prior to 2008, how many All-Stars did Tony Browne win?

1390 DJ Carey scored 4-32 in nine All-Ireland senior finals but in which three finals did he score those four goals?

1391 Brian Whelhan captained Offaly to an All-Ireland minor title in which season?

1392 With which club did Tipperary's Pat Fox play?

1393 Name the Cork forward from their All-Ireland three-in-a-row team from 1976-78 to score 3-35 in seven finals?

1394 With which Cork club did Kilkenny's Frank Cummins play?

1395 Antrim's Olcan McFetrdige was better known by which nickname?

1396 Offaly's Johnny Dooley played with which club?

1397 Name the Galway corner-forward who won All-Irelands in 1987 and 1988 and who subsequently had his career cut short through a nasty ear injury?

1398 Prior to 2008, Dan Shanahan was the first player to win the Texaco Hurler of the Year award in 2007 from a team which hadn't won an All-Ireland title since which Cork player?

1399 Name the Clare player who made his debut in the 1972 Munster final and who also played in the 1986 Munster final?

1400 Wexford's George O'Connor had the unique distinction of winning a medal in his first game in Croke Park and in his last game in Croke Park. He won an All-Ireland medal in his last game but which medal did he win in his first game?

GENERAL KNOWLEDGE

1401 Name the Kerry footballer who narrowly missed an equalising point in the dying moments of the 2002 All-Ireland final against Armagh?

1402 Who scored Limerick's only goal in the 2007 All-Ireland hurling final?

1403 With almost the last puck of the 2006 All-Ireland hurling semi-final, Donal Óg Cusack stopped a long-range free from going over the bar for the equalising point. Name the freetaker?

1404 Who was the first county to win both hurling and football All-Ireland senior titles?

1405 Former Dublin football manager Paul Caffrey is more commonly known by which nickname?

1406 Where are the four Provincial Councils' offices located?

1407 True or False? Cork have reached more Munster hurling finals than Tipperary this decade.

1408 Who was the first captain to bring the new Sam Maguire Cup to Ulster?

1409 Before the All-Stars were officially formalised in 1971, which now defunct magazine sponsored the selection of All-Star teams from 1963 to 1967 (inclusive) in both hurling and football?

ANSWERS PAGE 234

1410 In the last 40 years, three goalkeepers have captained teams to the Sam Maguire. Name them?

1411 Pat Spillane played in ten All-Ireland finals with Kerry but in which two finals did he appear as a substitute?

1412 How many Leinster counties reached a provincial senior football final this decade?

1413 Brian Murphy, who played as a goalkeeper with Dublin in the 2003 and 2004 senior football championship, won an All-Ireland minor medal with which county?

1414 With which two clubs does Clare's Colin Lynch play hurling and football?

1415 Prior to 2008, name the only four counties to never have had a representative on an International Rules Football squad?

1416 Prior to 2008 name the player who recorded the highest score by an individual footballer on a losing team in an All-Ireland senior football final?

1417 Name the player who recorded the highest score by an individual hurler on a losing team in an All-Ireland hurling final?

1418 Name the player who wasn't named on the programme, who didn't start the game, who didn't finish the game, but who scored the decisive goal in an All-Ireland senior hurling final in the last 30 years?

1419 Name the Dublin player who scored six goals in the 1960 Leinster championship against Longford, a total not equalled until 42 years later when Fermanagh's Rory Gallagher got 3-9 against Monaghan?

1420 In the Gaelic Football senior championship, name the first player to receive a red card and be sent off?

MONAGHAN GENERAL KNOWLEDGE

1421 Who captained Monaghan in the 2007 Ulster senior football final?

1422 After Castleblayney Faughs, which club holds the most county senior football titles?

1423 Who managed Monaghan to the 1999 Ulster U-21 title?

1424 Who did Monaghan defeat in the 1985 National League final?

1425 Which county defeated Monaghan in the 1979 All-Ireland senior football semi-final?

1426 Who won Monaghan's first football All-Star award?

1427 Which club has won the most Monaghan county senior hurling titles?

1428 Which Monaghan club were the first club to defeat Crossmaglen Rangers in a championship match in three years in the 2000 Ulster club championship?

1429 Prior to 2008, when did Monaghan last contest an Ulster minor football final?

1430 Scotstown contested five Ulster club football finals but how many did they win?

1431 Monaghan reached the Centenary Football final in 1984 but which county defeated them?

1432 Apart from Pat McEnaney, name the only other Monaghan man to referee an All-Ireland senior football final in the last 30 years?

1433 In which year did Clontibret O'Neill's reach their only Ulster club football final (it was in the last 15 years)?

1434 Name the former Tipperary All-Ireland hurling medal winner who played with Monaghan in their 1997 All-Ireland junior hurling success?

1435 Name the former Monaghan footballer who won a Clare county senior football title with Lissycasey in 2007?

1436 Name the former All-Ireland Colleges hurling medallist with St Flannan's College, Ennis, who played with the Monaghan hurlers in the 2008 Ulster hurling championship?

1437 Name the former Monaghan player who was the trainer with Liam Austin when they were sensationally forced to quit with Cavan in 1998?

1438 In which year did Monaghan contest their only All-Ireland minor football final?

1439 Monaghan won their two Ulster senior hurling titles in successive years – which years?

1440 Which year in the last 20 years did Monaghan not compete in the Ulster minor football championship because of hassle with the Leaving Certificate?

A HURLING HISTORY

1441 Tipperary and Galway contested the first ever All-Ireland hurling final but which clubs represented those counties?

1442 Tipperary won three All-Ireland titles between 1895 and 1898 but name the famous club which represented the county in those finals?

1443 Kilkenny were the first county in the 1900s to win three All-Irelands in a row (between 1911-13) but one of those titles (1911) was decided in the boardroom after the Munster champions refused to replay the final which was postponed owing to the state of the pitch. Who were the Munster champions that year, which caused all the controversy?

1444 Jim (Andy) O Hehir (father of legendary commentator Micheal) trained which hurling team to win an All-Ireland title in the 1910s?

1445 'Gah' Aherne and 'Hawker' Grady won All-Ireland medals with which county in the 1920s?

1446 The 1931 All-Ireland hurling final, regarded by many historians as possibly the greatest All-Ireland final ever, went to three games. Which two counties contested the final that year?

1447 Of the three All-Ireland titles Limerick won between 1934 and 1940, the legendary Mick Mackey captained them to how many of those titles?

1448 Who captained Cork to the 1944 All-Ireland title, becoming the only hurler in history to captain a team to four All-Irelands in a row?

1449 Wexford contested four All-Ireland hurling finals in the 1950s but how many did they win?

1450 In how many All-Ireland finals did Christy Ring play with Cork in the 1950s – four, five or six?

1451 Which county did Waterford defeat after a replay in the 1959 All-Ireland final to record only their second All-Ireland title?

1452 The legendary Tipperary full-back line (all three played in the 1950s and 1960s) of John Doyle, Mick Maher and Kieran Carey were known by which term?

1453 Tipperary contested eight All-Ireland finals between 1958-68 but how many did they win – four, five or six?

1454 True or False? When Kilkenny reached five All-Ireland finals in-a-row between 1971-75, they became the first county in history to reach five finals in a row (not including when clubs could represent the county)?

1455 Who coached Cork to their three All-Irelands in a row between 1976-78?

1456 Who managed Galway to the 1980 All-Ireland title?

1457 Who captained Offaly to their first All-Ireland title in 1981?

ANSWERS PAGE 234

1458 When Clare won the All-Ireland title in 1995, it was their first title in how many years?

1459 Name the player from the Wexford squad of 1996, whose father had won All-Irelands with the county in 1955 and 1956?

1460 When Cork halted Kilkenny's quest for three in a row in 2004, it was the first goalless All-Ireland final since which year?

FOOTBALL GOALSCORERS OVER THE LAST 35 YEARS

1461 Name the only player to score in both national finals (All-Ireland and league) in 1977?

1462 Who scored Armagh's only goal in the 2002 All-Ireland football final?

1463 Prior to 2008, name the last player to score three goals in an All-Ireland football final?

1464 Name the player who scored 3-2 in the 2005 All-Ireland U-21 final?

1465 Name the Meath player who scored goals in the 1996 All-Ireland semi-final and the 2007 All-Ireland quarter-final?

1466 Who scored Cavan's only goal in the 1997 Ulster final?

1467 Prior to 2008, the fifth highest goalscorer in Ulster history is a Derry player who is still currently playing. Name him?

1468 Name the player who scored 4-5 in a league game against Galway in 2004?

1469 Name the Armagh player who scored 13 goals in championship between 1984 and 2000?

1470 Prior to 2008, no other player had scored as many goals (five) in All-Ireland semi-finals as which Kerry player?

1471 Name the Down player who scored four goals in just four championship matches in 2004?

1472 Name the Meath player who hit three goals in the 2001 drawn and replayed All-Ireland quarter-finals against Westmeath?

1473 Name the legendary Offaly player who packed 88 goals in a seven-year career?

1474 Prior to 2008, which Kerry player became the first man since Jimmy Keaveney in 1977 to find the net in both national finals in the one year – league and championship?

1475 Name the Kerry player to score goals in 27 of his 48 championship games?

1476 Prior to 2008, name the Armagh modern player who had scored 17 championship goals, the same number as Sean O'Neill and Peter Donohue?

1477 Along with Joe Kavanagh, name the only other non-Kerryman to score goals in two All-Ireland finals in the last 35 years?

1478 Name the Kerry player who netted the decisive goals in three league finals as well as being on target in three All-Ireland finals?

ANSWERS PAGE 235

1479 Name the only player from the last 15 years to have completed a grand slam of scoring at least one goal in a league semi-final and final and an All-Ireland semi-final and final?

1480 Name the legendary Cork player who scored a goal with each of his four touches in the 1975 Railway Cup final for Munster?

OFFALY GENERAL KNOWLEDGE

1481 Name the Offaly player who played in the 2007 football championship after transferring from Westmeath?

1482 The son of a former All-Ireland winning Offaly captain made his debut in the 2008 hurling championship against Laois. Name him?

1483 Who managed the Offaly footballers to the 2004 Division Two National League title?

1484 Who scored Offaly's two goals in the 1998 All-Ireland final win against Kilkenny?

1485 Offaly hurler Brian Carroll won an All-Ireland Colleges title with which college in 2000?

1486 As part of an agreement years ago between the Tipperary and Offaly county boards, Moneygall is inside the Offaly border but the club plays its hurling in Tipperary. Name the club which is situated within the Tipperary border but plays its club hurling in Offaly?

1487 Four Offaly players were selected on the first All-Star team in 1971. Name two of them?

1488 Name the three Offaly goalscorers in the 1994 All-Ireland final?

1489 Name the only Offaly player in the top 20 all-time senior hurling championship scorers?

ANSWERS PAGE 235

1490 True or False? Offaly have won three Leinster senior hurling titles in a row just once in their history.

1491 Who captained Offaly to their first All-Ireland minor hurling title in 1986?

1492 Which player was at the centre of the controversy – he was sent off in an U-21 game but was introduced as a late sub in a subsequent league game with Longford while still under suspension – which saw Offaly deducted points in the 2007 National Football league and which ultimately saw them relegated to Division Four?

1493 Which Kilkenny club did Birr defeat to record their first Leinster club title in 1991?

1494 Name the only Offaly footballer selected as an All-Star in 1997?

1495 When Offaly were going for three All-Ireland football titles in a row in 1973, who defeated them in that year's All-Ireland semi-final?

1496 Name three of the four Offaly hurlers to play in All-Ireland semi-finals in the 1980s, 1990s and 2000s?

1497 Name the Offaly All-Ireland medal winner from 1981, who played with Seir Kieran in the 2000 Offaly county final (played in 2001)?

1498 In which year did a dispute arise with the Offaly footballers, which was connected with an All-Stars trip to San Francisco, when players were pushing for £1,000 from the county board to be added to their lavish per diem of $6?

1499 Birr had only one representative on the starting 15 which won the county's first Leinster title in 1980. He was full-back. Name him?

1500 Name the two Offaly players who won Leinster senior football medals in 1997 and who also played on the Offaly minor hurling and football teams which reached the 1989 All-Ireland finals?

CLUBCALL 2

Name the county of the following clubs

1501 Burgess

1502 Turloughmore

1503 Newcestown

1504 Galtee Gaels

1505 Tubberclare

1506 Loughmacrory

1507 Tubber

1508 Ballydurn

1509 Ballylongford

1510 Lusmagh

1511 Clane

1512 Blackhall Gaels

1513 Naomh Olaf

1514 Ballylinan

1515 Belcoo

1516 Legan Sarsfields

1517 Marshalstown

1518 Hollymount

1519 Granemore

1520 Naomh Moninne

ANSWERS PAGE 235

GENERAL KNOWLEDGE

1521 Only four players have won All-Stars in both hurling and football. Name three of them?

1522 What new experimental rule (similar to rugby) was brought in for the secondary competitions (e.g O'Byrne Cup) in 2005 but was subsequently dropped before the league began?

1523 Name the three Leinster counties to have won hurling and football All-Ireland titles?

1524 Name the only county not to have won a senior football championship game outside its own county grounds in the last 38 years?

1525 Two men who have refereed All-Ireland senior football finals in the last 30 years have run for the GAA presidency. Name them?

1526 In 1976 and 2008, Kerry defeated Kildare in All-Ireland U-21 finals and two Kerry players from the 1976 team had sons on the 2008 team. Name the fathers and sons?

1527 What was historic about the 2008 Ulster senior hurling championship?

1528 In the last 15 years, name the three counties to have won an All-Ireland senior football title without having won an All-Ireland minor or U-21 title in the previous ten years?

1529 Prior to 2008, name the last player to captain a football team to their third All-Ireland senior title in a row?

ANSWERS PAGE 235

1530 Prior to 2008, name the last player to captain a hurling team to their third All-Ireland senior title in a row?

1531 Name the only Kilkenny hurler to play in eight All-Ireland finals between 1998 and 2007?

1532 Of the 12 highest scorers in All-Ireland hurling semi-finals between 1997 and 2007, one of those players was a defender. Name him?

1533 With which club does Dublin's Barry Cahill play?

1534 Which college won the Leinster Colleges Senior football title for the first time in history in 2008?

1535 Name the Waterford club to win nine All-Ireland club ladies' football titles in ten years between 1989 and 1998?

1536 True or False? Prior to 2008, an All-Ireland hurling and football three-in-a-row in the same year has only been achieved once.

1537 Name the only Kerry player to have won minor, U-21 and more than one senior All-Ireland medal on the field of play in the last 15 years?

1538 Name the father and son who were involved with the Meath footballers as a selector and player in 2007 and 2008?

1539 Kerry footballer, Paul Galvin, won Munster club football Player of the Year with which club in the last ten years?

1540 Prior to 2008, only three counties had failed to produce a representative in a provincial club football final. Name two of them?

ANSWERS PAGE 235

ROSCOMMON GENERAL KNOWLEDGE

1541 Who managed Roscommon to the 2008 Connacht U-21 football final?

1542 Name the Roscommon player who famously broke the crossbar during Roscommon's Connacht final clash with Mayo in 1992?

1543 Who took over as Roscommon manager after Tommy Carr stepped down in 2005?

1544 Who captained Roscommon to the 2007 Nicky Rackard Cup title?

1545 True or False? Roscommon reached three League football semi-finals in a row between 2000-02?

1546 Who captained St Brigid's to the 2006 Connacht club title?

1547 Name the former football All-Star who played in the 2002 Connacht club hurling final with Four Roads?

1548 Tony McManus – the last Roscommon footballer to captain a successful Sigerson Cup winning team – led which college to success in 1979?

1549 Name the two Roscommon brothers to win All-Star awards?

1550 Which county defeated Roscommon in the 1999 All-Ireland U-21 football semi-final?

1551 When Four Roads won the 1988 Connacht club hurling title, which Galway club did they defeat in the final?

1552 Name the Clann na nGael manager who led the club to six Connacht club titles in a row between 1985 and 1990?

1553 How many All-Ireland club football finals did Clann na nGael lose?

1554 Name the Roscommon player who captained the county in the 1962 All-Ireland football final and who also played Railway Cup hurling for Connacht on three occasions?

1555 Name the only Roscommon player to be part of the Connacht hurling squad that contested the 2007 Interprovincial final?

1556 Name the two Roscommon players selected on the GAA's Centenary Football Team, comprising players who never won an All-Ireland senior medal?

1557 Who scored Roscommon's only goal in the 2007 Nicky Rackard Cup final?

1558 When Roscommon were going for three All-Ireland titles in a row in 1945, which county defeated them in that year's Connacht final?

1559 Roscommon won their first All-Ireland U-21 football title in which year?

1560 Who managed Roscommon to the 1991 Connacht football title?

ANSWERS PAGE 235

TOP TEN NUMBER OF SENIOR HURLING CHAMPIONSHIP APPEARANCES BY SETS OF BROTHERS, PLUS THE TOP TEN HIGHEST SCORING SIBLINGS IN CHAMPIONSHIP HISTORY

All prior to 2008

1561 Which set of three brothers (who played up until ten years ago) are the highest scoring siblings in championship history with a total of 27-301?

1562 Which set of brothers (they played up until ten years ago) have played the highest number of games in the championship with 113 appearances?

1563 Which set of Tipperary brothers are the second highest championship scorers in history?

1564 The three Henderson brothers from Kilkenny have played the second highest number of championship games in history but which of those brothers had the most number of caps with 40 – Pat, Ger or John?

1565 The Rackard brothers from Wexford are the third highest championship scorers with a combined total of 60-101. But which brother – Nicky, Billy or Bobby – made the most championship appearances?

1566 The Rackards have played the third highest number of championship games in history but name the fourth Rackard – apart from Nicky, Billy and Bobby – who also played for Wexford?

1567 Name the Limerick set of brothers who are the fourth highest championship scorers in history with 44-91 in 85 games?

1568 Name the three brothers (who all played up until five years ago) who have the fourth highest number of championship appearances by sets of brothers?

1569 Name the two Offaly brothers who hit 17-171 in 54 games?

1570 How many of the four Fennelly brothers, Ger, Liam, Sean and Kevin – who have played the fifth highest number of championship games in history – captained Kilkenny in All-Ireland finals?

1571 The Connolly brothers from Galway are the sixth highest championship scorers for a set of brothers in championship. But name the other brother apart from John, Joe and Michael to play for Galway?

1572 Dan, John, Martin and Pat Quigley all played for Wexford in the 1970 All-Ireland final but name the fifth Quigley brother who also played championship for Wexford?

1573 Name the only four siblings to score in hurling championship history?

1574 Which set of Clare brothers have played the seventh highest number of championship games (collectively)?

1575 Name the two Wexford brothers who bagged 42-60 in 64 championship games?

ANSWERS PAGE 236

1576 Johnny, Paddy, Mick and Tommy Leahy played a collective total of 95 championship games with which county?

1577 Which of the four Fennelly brothers – Ger, Liam, Kevin and Sean – never scored in championship?

1578 Name the three Doyle brothers who played 92 times for Kilkenny?

1579 Name the two Tipperary brothers (one of whom played in the 2008 championship) who scored 8-135 between them in 71 games prior to the 2008 championship?

1580 Prior to 2008, the set of brothers with the tenth highest number of championship appearances (85) were from Limerick. Name them?

FOOTBALLERS WHO HAVE PLAYED IN ALL-IRELAND FINALS OVER THE LAST 20 YEARS

Match the player to his county

1581 John Miskella

1582 Colin Holmes

1583 Darren O'Sullivan

1584 Stephen Stack

1585 Padraig Graven

1586 Brian Murray

1587 Barry Coffey

1588 Liam Harnan

1589 Damien Cassidy

1590 Kevin Cahill

1591 Dermot Geraghty

1592 Paddy Moran

1593 Paul Higgins

1594 Alan Keane

1595 Donal Curtis

1596 Seamus McCallan

1597 Barry McGowan

1598 Mick Slocum

1599 Michael Fitzmaurice

1600 John Sheehan

ANSWERS PAGE 236

SLIGO GENERAL KNOWLEDGE

1601 Which county did Sligo defeat in the 2008 Nicky Rackard Cup final?

1602 True or False? Philip Greene, goalkeeper on the Sligo team which won the 2007 Connacht football title, never played underage football for Sligo as a goalkeeper.

1603 Which Sligo club contested five Connacht football finals between 1979-85?

1604 Name the only Sligo player to play International Rules?

1605 Who won Sligo's first All-Star award?

1606 Which club won ten Sligo senior hurling titles in a row between 1995-2004?

1607 Which member of the 2007 Sligo team which won the Connacht title is a professional musician?

1608 True or False? Mickey Kearns, who was a well-known referee after his playing days, refereed an All-Ireland senior football final.

1609 Which former Sligo player took over as caretaker manager and led Sligo to the 2004 Tommy Murphy Cup title?

1610 When Sligo recorded their memorable win against Tyrone in the 2002 football qualifiers, who scored their only goal?

1611 Which club won their first county senior hurling title in 2005?

1612 Who captained Sligo to the 2008 Nicky Rackford Cup final?

1613 Name the former All-Ireland senior medal winner with Galway from 1980 who managed the Sligo hurlers in 2008?

1614 Name two of the three Sligo players to win All-Stars?

1615 Which club defeated St Mary's in the 1984 Connacht club football final?

1616 Which county did Sligo defeat in the 1922 All-Ireland football semi-final?

1617 Although Sligo won the 1922 All-Ireland football semi-final, how come they never got the opportunity to play in that year's All-Ireland final?

1618 Name the former Mayo footballer who managed Curry to the 2003 Connacht club football final?

1619 He was a former priest who played with Limerick in the 1980 All-Ireland final and he managed the Sligo hurlers for a brief period in 2003. Name him?

1620 Name the Sligo player who scored 3-8 against London in the 1978 Connacht championship?

ANSWERS PAGE 236

MOST PROLIFIC HURLING GOALSCORING SEQUENCES AND LEADING HURLING GOALSCORERS IN ALL-IRELAND SENIOR FINALS BETWEEN 1930-2007

1621 Name the legendary player who scored 52 goals in 26 games between 1950-56?

1622 Ted O'Sullivan scored 22 goals in 13 games for which county between 1939-43?

1623 The leading goalscorer in All-Ireland senior hurling finals is a Limerick man who hit eight goals in four finals between 1933-36. Name him?

1624 Name the Offaly hurler who scored 22 goals in 13 games between 1962-69?

1625 Name the Wexford player who hit 23 goals in 16 games between 1967-73?

1626 Name the Laois player who hit 16 goals in 12 games between 1952-60?

1627 How many All-Ireland final appearances did Eddie Keher make– 10, 11 or 12?

1628 Tim Flood scored 16 goals in 13 games for Wexford between 1952-56 but in which year's All-Ireland final did he score a goal – 1954, 1955 or 1956?

1629 Tony Doran scored six goals in how many All-Ireland finals for Wexford?

1630 Name the Cork player who hit 12 goals in ten games between 1972-75?

ANSWERS PAGE 236

1631 Name the Kilkenny player with the most prolific goalscoring sequence, scoring 13 goals in 11 championship matches?

1632 Nicky Rackard scored five goals in how many All-Ireland finals for Wexford?

1633 Christy Ring scored 14 goals in 12 consecutive games but in which year's All-Ireland final did Art Foley make his famous save from Ring?

1634 Name the Limerick player to hit 17 goals in 15 games between 1979-84?

1635 Name the Tipperary player who scored five goals in six All-Ireland finals between 1961-68?

1636 Joe Kelly scored 16 goals in 15 games between 1944-47 for which county?

1637 Name the modern hurler who scored goals in seven successive Munster hurling championship matches between 2004 and 2007?

1638 Name the Cork player to score five goals in seven All-Ireland finals between 1972-84?

1639 In how many of his ten All-Ireland Senior Hurling Championship final appearances (including 1959 as a teenage sub) did Kilkenny's Eddie Keher score a goal – six, seven or eight?

1640 Who was the last man to score three goals in an All-Ireland Senior Hurling Championship final?

ANSWERS PAGE 236

MATCH THE HURLER TO HIS CLUB

1641 Brian O'Connell (Clare)

1642 Keith Rossiter (Wexford)

1643 Conor O'Mahony (Tipperary)

1644 Michael Walsh (Waterford)

1645 Noel Hickey (Kilkenny)

1646 Timmy McCarthy (Cork)

1647 Damian Reale (Limerick)

1648 Ger Farragher (Galway)

1649 Ger Oakley (Offaly)

1650 David O'Callaghan (Dublin)

1651 Pat Mullaney (Laois)

1652 Ciaran Herron (Antrim)

1653 Paul Braniff (Down)

1654 Liam Hinphey (Derry)

1655 Enda Loughlin (Westmeath)

1656 Mike O'Brien (Limerick)

1657 Shane Brick (Kerry)

1658 Paul McCormack (Armagh)

1659 Jonathon Clancy (Clare)

1660 Willie O'Dwyer (Kilkenny)

ANSWERS PAGE 236

TIPPERARY GENERAL KNOWLEDGE

1661 When Tipperary defeated Cork in the 2008 Munster hurling championship, it was the first time Tipp had defeated Cork in Páirc Uí Chaoimh since which year – 1921, 1923 or 1925?

1662 Who defeated Tipperary in the 2008 Division Four National Football League final?

1663 The Tipperary hurling coach in 2008, Eamonn O'Shea, won an All-Ireland club medal with which club?

1664 Name the Tipperary hurler who played in the 2008 Munster hurling final, 30 years after his father won an All-Star in 1978?

1665 Who managed the Tipperary footballers in the 2004 championship, when they withdrew from the All-Ireland qualifiers over a row with the county board over club fixtures?

1666 In which year did Brian Gaynor, son of Len, play in an All-Ireland minor hurling final?

1667 Which county defeated Tipperary in the 1995 All-Ireland minor football semi-final?

1668 In how many Munster hurling finals did Nicky English play (including replays) – nine, ten or eleven?

1669 Who managed Tipperary to the 2002 Munster senior football final, which they lost to Cork after a replay?

1670 In which year did Declan Browne win a National hurling league medal with Tipp?

1671 Which club had four starting players on the Tipperary team which reached the 2008 Munster hurling final?

1672 Which Tipperary player scored 2-12 against Galway in the 1971 All-Ireland hurling semi-final?

1673 Name the player who captained Tipperary to the 1993 Munster senior hurling title but who was subsequently dropped for the All-Ireland semi-final against Galway?

1674 Who are the only Tipperary school to win an All-Ireland Colleges title?

1675 Name the Tipperary player to play International Rules in 1990?

1676 Ardán Uí Riain, the new stand in Thurles, was first opened in which year – 1980, 1981 or 1982?

1677 Name the hurling goalkeeper who replaced Ken Hogan in 1994, winning a National League medal that season, a year before Brendan Cummins took over as number one?

1678 Name the player who got a high-court injunction to allow him to to play in the 1994 Munster football final?

1679 Jimmy Doyle captained Tipperary to the 1962 All-Ireland title but he was injured 11 minutes into the second-half of the final. Which player accepted the Liam MacCarthy Cup?

1680 When Paul Byrne came on as a substitute in the 1971 All-Ireland final, what unique distinction did he carve for a Tipperary-man?

GAA FAMILIES

1681 Name the three brothers who were part of the Dublin football squad in 2008?

1682 Name the two Monaghan brothers nominated for All-Stars in 2007?

1683 Name the two brothers who played in the 2006 All-Ireland final for Mayo?

1684 Name the two sets of brothers who played for Waterford in their 2004 and 2007 Munster hurling final wins?

1685 Which family had four brothers on an inter-county football panel in 2008?

1686 Name the last father and son to win an All-Ireland senior football title with the same team as manager and player (who was on the squad)?

1687 Name the two brothers to captain their club in All-Ireland club hurling finals over the last ten years?

1688 Name the only two brothers to captain their club to an All-Ireland club football title (they managed it in the last 15 years)?

1689 Richie and Matt Connor won All-Ireland football medals with Offaly in 1982 but name their brother who won an All-Ireland medal with the county in 1971 and 1972?

1690 Name the last two brothers to captain their county in an All-Ireland hurling final?

ANSWERS PAGE 237

1691 Name the last father and son to win an All-Ireland senior football title with the same team as manager and player (on the field of play)?

1692 Name the father (who made his championship debut as a manager) and son who were involved together in the 2008 hurling championship?

1693 Prior to 2008, name the last two brothers to captain their county to an All-Ireland hurling title?

1694 Name the last manager to manage teams including his sons in two different counties?

1695 Name the last father and son to win All-Ireland senior hurling medals as a manager and player with the same team?

1696 They were both priests who played together on the same half-forward line in an All-Ireland senior hurling final in the last 30 years. Name them?

1697 Name the only set of twins to play together in the 2008 football championship?

1698 Name the last set of three brothers who each captained their county in an All-Ireland hurling final (it happened in the last 35 years)?

1699 Name the only three brothers to play International Rules football?

1700 Name the two brothers who managed teams against each other in Division One of the National Hurling League in the last ten years?

ANSWERS PAGE 237

OUTSTANDING HURLING AND FOOTBALL GOALS OF THE LAST 10 YEARS

1701 Peter Canavan scored Tyrone's only goal in the 2005 All-Ireland final against Kerry but name the Tyrone forward who provided him with the final pass for that goal?

1702 Name the Wexford forward who scored the goal in the dying seconds of the 2004 Leinster semi-final against Kilkenny, which Wexford won by two points?

1703 Colm Cooper scored the opening goal of the 2007 All-Ireland final after getting in a sublime punch to a dropping ball between the advancing keeper and another Cork defender. Name the Cork goalkeeper?

1704 Name the Galway player who picked the ball up 45 metres from goal in the second-half of the 2008 National League hurling final against Tipperary, and beat three men before lashing the ball to the net?

1705 DJ Carey scored an outstanding goal in the 1999 All-Ireland semi-final, when he caught a high ball in the second-half, raced away from two defenders before drilling the ball to the net. Which county did Kilkenny beat that day?

1706 Name the Sligo player who scored an outstanding and decisive goal in the 2007 Connacht football final?

1707 Name the Cork player who scored the only goal in the 1999 Munster final against Clare after Seanie McGrath had made a one-handed flick to direct the ball back across the goal?

ANSWERS PAGE 237

1708 Dan Shanahan scored a class goal from a ball which he struck from the ground in the 2007 All-Ireland quarter-final against Cork. But was that goal scored in the drawn or replayed match?

1709 Name the Galway defender who scored a superb goal in the 2000 All-Ireland football final replay after a sweeping move?

1710 Limerick's Andrew O'Shaughnessy scored a classic goal in the 2007 All-Ireland semi-final against Waterford, when after picking up the ball nearly 40 metres from goal, he burned his marker before driving the ball to the net from an acute angle. O'Shaughnessy's marker was a former All-Ireland Colleges medal winner with him in St Colman's Fermoy. Name him?

1711 Who scored Dublin's only goal against Armagh in the 2002 All-Ireland semi-final after an outstanding run through the centre before crashing his shot off the underside of the crossbar?

1712 In which year's Leinster hurling final did Henry Shefflin score an outstanding goal when he doubled on a pass from Martin Comerford as he was falling backwards?

1713 Name the Kilkenny forward who scored the county's only goal in the 2002 All-Ireland semi-final against Tipperary after DJ Carey had split the defence open with a brilliant move?

ANSWERS PAGE 237

1714 In which year's championship did Joe Deane score a brilliant goal against Limerick with a flick from a long-range delivery?

1715 The second-best goal of the 2005 football championship was a Steven McDonnell strike against Laois in the All-Ireland quarter-final. The goal was made by a superb knock-down from a long ball into McDonnell's path by which Armagh player?

1716 The only goal Tipperary scored in the 2002 Munster quarter-final against Clare was a rocket to the top corner hit by which player?

1717 Name the Offaly player who scored a goal from 25 metres in the 2003 drawn Leinster football quarter-final against Laois?

1718 Name the player who got Galway's goal in the second half of the 2001 All-Ireland hurling final, which he struck from almost the endline?

1719 Name the Waterford forward who scored a super goal against Cork, with a shot struck from the ground that nearly took Donal Og Cusack's head off, in the 2005 Munster semi-final?

1720 Name the Galway substitute who turned the 2001 All-Ireland semi-final against Derry with a superb goal?

ANSWERS PAGE 237

TYRONE GENERAL KNOWLEDGE

1721 Name the Tyrone player who captained Ulster to the 2007 Interprovincial title?

1722 Name the Tyrone footballer who was a key member of the St Pat's Dungannon backroom team which won the 2008 All-Ireland Colleges football title?

1723 Name the former successful Ulster title winning manager who managed the Tyrone hurlers in the 2008 Ulster championship?

1724 Who scored Tyrone's only goal in the 1986 All-Ireland football final against Kerry?

1725 Name the Tyrone defender who made the famous late block to deny Steven McDonnell a goal in the 2003 All-Ireland final?

1726 Name the Tyrone club which won the 2005 Ulster club minor hurling championship?

1727 Which club won their first senior football county title in 2003?

1728 Errigal Ciaran are the only Tyrone club to win an Ulster club title but name two of the three other Tyrone clubs to contest an Ulster final?

1729 Who managed Tyrone to successive All-Ireland football titles in 1991 and 1992?

1730 Which club has won the most Tyrone county senior hurling titles?

ANSWERS PAGE 237

1731 Name the 19-year-old who captained Tyrone to their first Ulster title in 1956?

1732 In which year did Tyrone win their first Ulster senior ladies' senior football title (it was in the last ten years)?

1733 In which town is the club called Sigersons?

1734 Who was the first Tyrone player to captain Ulster to Interprovincial success in 1984?

1735 Who captained Tyrone in the 1997 All-Ireland minor final?

1736 Name the first Tyrone hurler to be selected on an Ulster Railway Cup team in 1995, which narrowly lost that year's final to Munster?

1737 After Finbarr McConnell stepped down in 2001 and before John Devine established himself on the team in 2003, who was the goalkeeper for the 2002 National League success and that year's Ulster championship?

1738 Name the only Tyrone club to play in an All-Ireland senior Camogie final (it was in the last 20 years)?

1739 The late Paul McGirr, who was tragically killed during an Ulster minor game in 1997 against Armagh, has which All-Ireland trophy named after him?

1740 Name the only Tyrone man to win the All-Ireland Poc Fada title?

ANSWERS PAGE 237

GENERAL KNOWLEDGE

1741 With which club does Kerry goalkeeper Diarmuid Murphy play?

1742 In which year was the back door first introduced for the All-Ireland minor hurling championship?

1743 In which year was the back door first introduced for the All-Ireland minor football championship?

1744 Name the former All-Ireland winning Dublin footballer who later played senior hurling with Kerry?

1745 In which US city was the 2006 Ulster hurling final played?

1746 The player who has played the most Leinster senior hurling championship games (36) is a Wexford player who lined out in the 2008 championship. Name him?

1747 In the 2000 hurling league, how was the game started in the first and second halves?

1748 In which year was the experimental rule brought in during the football league where a hand-pass had to be followed by a fist-pass – 1994, 1995 or 1996?

1749 Who managed the Cavan footballers in the 2008 football championship?

1750 The first full-time GAA coaching officer won All-Ireland hurling medals with Tipperary in 1989 and 1991. Name him?

ANSWERS PAGE 237

1751 Prior to 2008, name the teams and the year when two teams from the same province contested an All-Ireland minor football final?

1752 Prior to 2008, name the teams and the year when two teams from the same province contested an All-Ireland minor hurling final?

1753 Name the last All-Ireland captain to lose an All-Ireland after captaining a winning one?

1754 Name the Galway hurling goalkeeper from the last five years to play championship hurling without having previously played a single league game?

1755 Pad Joe Whelahan played in two All-Ireland club hurling finals with which club?

1756 In the last ten years, there has only been one occasion when the All-Ireland club hurling final has taken place after the All-Ireland club football final. Which year?

1757 Name the former Limerick hurler, who played in the 1994 All-Ireland final, who managed the Kerry hurlers in 2008?

1758 In the 2008 football championship, two brothers played at the same venue on the same day but for different counties. Name them?

1759 When was the last time that the Leinster hurling semi-finals were played outside the province (it was in the last ten years)?

1760 Name the only player to play in Munster senior and Leinster senior football finals in the last 20 years?

ANSWERS PAGE 237

FIRSTS

1761 Pat Spillane won the first of his nine All-Star awards in which year – 1975, 1976 or 1977?

1762 The All-Ireland minor hurling championship was first played in which year – 1926, 1927 or 1928?

1763 The Railway Cup (both hurling and football) was first played in which year – 1925, 1926 or 1927?

1764 The All-Ireland club championships were initiated in which year (when the first finals were played) – 1970, 1971, 1972?

1765 Who were the first winners of the Tommy Murphy Cup in 2004?

1766 The All-Ireland U-21 championships began in which year – 1964, 1965, 1966?

1767 The All-Ireland minor football championship was first played in which year – 1927, 1928 or 1929?

1768 DJ Carey won the first of his nine All-Star awards in which year – 1990, 1991 or 1992?

1769 The Liam MacCarthy Cup was first presented in which year – 1922, 1923 or 1924?

1770 The first All-Ireland ladies' senior football final was played in which year – 1972, 1973 or 1974?

ANSWERS PAGE 238

1771 Who were the first winners of the Nicky Rackard Cup?

1772 The Hogan Cup (All-Ireland Colleges Football) was first played in which year – 1945, 1946 or 1947?

1773 The National Hurling and Football Leagues were first played when – 1924/25, 1925/1926 or 1926/27?

1774 The All-Ireland Poc Fada final was first held in which year – 1960, 1961 or 1962?

1775 The Croke Cup (All-Ireland Colleges Hurling) was first played in which year – 1944, 1945 or 1946?

1776 Which national hurling competition was played for the first time in 1911/12?

1777 What was the first national Camogie championship ever played?

1778 Teams were reduced to 15 a side from which year – 1913, 1914 or 1915?

1779 The first All-Ireland final played in Jones' Road was in which year – 1893, 1894 or 1895?

1780 When was a goal first made equal to three points – 1894, 1895 or 1896?

WATERFORD GENERAL KNOWLEDGE

1781 Name the four Waterford players selected as hurling All-Stars in 2007?

1782 Name three of the four Waterford clubs to have contested Munster club football finals?

1783 Name the three Waterford hurling selectors who stepped down along with Justin McCarthy in 2008?

1784 Dan Shanahan played in two Munster minor hurling finals in which years?

1785 Who is the only Waterford player to win a Munster senior hurling medal, a Munster U-21 football medal and an All-Star award?

1786 Who did Ballygunner defeat in the 2001 Munster club final to win their first provincial title?

1787 Which Waterford club took UCC (eventual winners) to a replay in the 1999 Munster club football championship?

1788 Name the former All-Ireland winning captain from Kilkenny, who firstly had to become a member of the Mount Sion club in order to take over as manager at the outset of 2008, and who subsequently had his tenure terminated by the club executive after Mount Sion lost their opening two games in the senior championship?

1789 Waterford hurler Brian Phelan goes by which nickname?

ANSWERS PAGE 238

1790 The Waterford minor hurling manager in 2008, Mick Mahoney, won a Munster club hurling medal with which club?

1791 Who won Waterford's first hurling All-Star?

1792 One of the De La Salle joint-coaches of the 2007 and 2008 All-Ireland winning sides played in the 1992 All-Ireland minor final as a 15-year-old. Name him?

1793 The father of a well-known Tipperary hurler managed the Waterford footballers earlier this decade. Name the manager?

1794 Name the Waterford player selected on the GAA's Centenary Hurling team, comprising players who never won an All-Ireland?

1795 Name the only Waterford player to win an Interprovincial (formerly Railway Cup medal) with the Munster footballers on the field of play in the last 30 years?

1796 Name the De La Salle player who scored the winning point in the 2008 All-Ireland Colleges final replay?

1797 Name the only Waterford footballer to start the 2007 Interprovincial football final?

1798 Name the Mount Sion player who won 15 county hurling medals?

1799 Prior to 2007, who was the last Waterford man to captain Munster to Interprovincial success?

1800 Who managed Waterford to the 1992 Munster minor title and the 1994 Munster U-21 title?

ANSWERS PAGE 238

NOTEWORTHY ACHIEVEMENTS AND RECORDS IN HURLING AND FOOTBALL

1801 How many Railway Cup medals did Christy Ring win with Munster – 16, 17 or 18?

1802 How many National League hurling medals did Tipperary's John Doyle win – 10, 11 or 12?

1803 Name the only Armagh player to start in their eight Ulster football finals (including the 2008 replay) between 1999 and 2008?

1804 The only player to have won eleven consecutive Munster senior medals was also selected on the GAA's Hurling Team of the Millennium. Name him?

1805 Which were the first family in which three members received All-Star awards?

1806 After Noel Skehan (who won nine All-Ireland medals), name the only Kilkenny senior hurler with eight All-Ireland medals?

1807 Name the hurler who scored a colossal combined total of 13-11 in the 1954 Leinster final against Dublin and All-Ireland semi-final against Antrim?

1808 True or False? Of the ten Munster senior hurling medals won by Cork's Jimmy Barry-Murphy, he won those ten medals in two sequences of five-in-a-row.

ANSWERS PAGE 238

1809 Name the only player to figure in All-Ireland minor and senior finals in the same year?

1810 Name the only hurler in the last five years to hit eight points from play on two occasions in the championship?

1811 Only three players have managed to win consecutive Texaco Footballer of the Year awards. Name two of them?

1812 Which family hold the unique record of All-Ireland senior football medals won by three generations in direct line?

1813 Which Kilkenny player won his tenth Leinster senior hurling medal in 2008?

1814 Name the player who holds the unique record of participation in six All-Ireland finals between 1949 and 1954 in two contrasting roles – player and referee?

1815 Name the Cork hurler who scored goals in eight consecutive Munster championship matches between 1983-86?

1816 Jimmy Doyle was the first hurler to play in four All-Ireland minor finals in a row (between 1954-57) but how many of those finals did he win?

1817 The legendary Cork trainer, Jim 'Tough' Barry, trained 14 All-Ireland winning teams between 1926 and 1954. Thirteen of those teams were from Cork but which county did he also train to All-Ireland hurling success in the 1930s?

ANSWERS PAGE 238

1818 Name the Kerry player, selected on the GAA's Football Team of the Millennium, who won 15 Munster football medals between 1931 and 1948?

1819 Name the three generations of All-Ireland winners beginning with the man who won senior hurling All-Irelands with Limerick in 1936 and 1940, whose son won eight All-Ireland football medals with Kerry between 1975 and 1986, and his grandson won an All-Ireland hurling medal with Clare in 1995?

1820 Name the only player to win five All-Ireland U-21 medals (in hurling and football)?

ANSWERS PAGE 238

HURLING ALL-STARS

1821 Name the goalkeeper on the 2007 All-Stars team?

1822 Name the two Kilkenny corner-backs selected on the 2007 All-Stars team?

1823 Name the only goalkeeper in the last ten years (prior to 2008) to win successive All-Stars?

1824 Name the two Limerick forwards chosen on the 2007 All-Stars team?

1825 Outside of Kilkenny, Waterford and Limerick, the only other county represented on the 2007 team was Tipperary. Name that player?

1826 Name the only Galway hurler to win three awards in the last ten years (prior to 2008)?

1827 Name the only two Clare player to win two All-Stars (prior to 2008) in the last ten years?

1828 In which two seasons did Tipperary's Eoin and Paul Kelly win All-Stars in the same year?

1829 Name the player who was selected as All-Star centre-back in 2005, despite only playing in the position during the last 20 minutes of one game that season?

1830 In which year (in the last ten years) did Waterford win three All-Stars for the first time?

ANSWERS PAGE 238

1831 In the last five years, which player won an All-Star award, 12 years after he had won his first award?

1832 Along with Brendan Cummins, name the other two Tipperary goalkeepers selected as All-Stars?

1833 In the last ten years, two players have won All-Stars in the half-back line and full-forward line. Name them?

1834 Name the only player to win six All-Stars in a row?

1835 Which county has won the most hurling All-Star awards?

1836 Which two players won five successive hurling All-Star awards between 1971–75?

1837 Apart from the Bonnars and Kellys, name the only other set of Tipperary brothers to win All-Stars?

1838 Name the only Cork hurler over the age of 30 to win three All-Stars in a row?

1839 On how many occasions have the National league champions been overlooked for an All-Star award – three, four or five?

1840 Prior to 2008, name the only hurler over the age of 30 to win successive All-Stars in the last 20 years?

ANSWERS PAGE 238

WESTMEATH GENERAL KNOWLEDGE

1841 Name the two players who lifted the Division 2 National Football league trophy after Westmeath's success in 2008?

1842 How many Division Two football titles have Westmeath won this decade?

1843 Former Westmeath player and manager Seamus Qualter, who managed Westmeath to Christy Ring Cup titles in 2005 and 2007, is a son of which former Galway player?

1844 Which county did Westmeath sensationally defeat in 1994 (when they emerged from Division Four) to advance to a National League football semi-final?

1845 Who captained Westmeath to the Division Two National League hurling title in 2008?

1846 Name the only Westmeath College to win an All-Ireland Colleges title?

1847 Name the player who played with Westmeath in the 2000 football championship and who was a selector the following year during Westmeath's run to the All-Ireland quarter-final?

1848 Name the former Offaly All-Ireland medal winner who managed Westmeath footballers in 2000 before Luke Dempsey took over?

ANSWERS PAGE 238

1849 On the GAA's Centenary Hurling Team, comprising players who never won an All-Ireland senior medal, name the only Westmeath player selected?

1850 Who captained Westmeath to the 2007 Christy Ring Cup title?

1851 Which Westmeath footballer plays his club football with Salthill/Knocknacarra in Galway?

1852 In the *Celebrity Bainisteoir* TV series filmed in 2008, Marty Whelan managed which Westmeath club to the title?

1853 Name the Westmeath football All-Star nominee in 2001 who subsequently transferred to Longford?

1854 When Westmeath defeated Offaly in the Leinster football championship in 2008, it was their first time defeating their rivals in Tullamore since which year – 1922, 1932 or 1942?

1855 Name two of the three Westmeath clubs to qualify for a Leinster club football final?

1856 What unusual event occurred at the official opening of Cusack Park, Mullingar in 1933?

1857 Which Westmeath footballer scored the goal of the season in the 2000 Leinster quarter-final against Laois, when he slalomed his way through the Laois defence from midfield before stitching the ball in the top corner of the net?

ANSWERS PAGE 239

1858 In which year did the late Eamonn Coleman from Derry play with Athlone when they recorded a famous victory against Walsh Island in the Leinster club championship – 1981, 1982 or 1983?

1859 Name the Westmeath hurler to score goals in both the 2005 and 2007 Christy Ring Cup finals?

1860 When Westmeath played Carlow in the 1999 Leinster championship, in the first championship game where yellow and red cards were implemented, how many players were sent off?

HURLING GENERAL KNOWLEDGE

1861 Name the Antrim hurling joint-managers who guided the team in the 2007 and 2008 championships?

1862 With which club does Galway's John Lee play?

1863 Who are the only two counties to appear in four All-Ireland hurling finals in a row over the last 30 years?

1864 Name the player who scored a combined total of 2-26 in an All-Ireland semi-final and final in the 1970s?

1865 Name the Galway goalkeeper who got man of the match in the 1980 All-Ireland final?

1866 Who is the only player in hurling history to hit over 50 goals in senior championship hurling?

1867 Former Kilkenny hurler, Liam O'Brien, went by which nickname?

1868 When was the last time that two All-Ireland hurling semi-finals were played at the same venue on the same day?

1869 Name the only hurler to captain two All-Ireland senior winning teams and to manage a county to an All-Ireland final?

1870 Every Kilkenny All-Ireland winning coach/manager since 1979 has come from the Kilkenny 1971-75 team. Name three of those four coach/managers?

ANSWERS PAGE 239

1871 Only three players have captained their counties to successive All-Ireland senior hurling titles. Name two of them?

1872 In 1990 and 1991, the Tipperary and Cork hurlers played exhibition games against the All-Stars in which famous Canadian sports arena?

1873 In how many All-Ireland finals did Cyril Farrell manage Galway?

1874 Only two players have managed to hit more than 45 goals in senior championship hurling, one of whom is Matty Power. With which two counties did Power play?

1875 In an All-Ireland Colleges final in 1995, Joe Deane and Kevin Broderick each scored three goals in an epic game. With which colleges were both players playing?

1876 The Irish middleweight boxing champion in 2008, Matthew Macklin, played underage divisional hurling with which county?

1877 Only three hurlers in history have managed to score goals in 12 consecutive championship games. Two were from Wexford and one was from Limerick. Name them?

1878 Who was the last hurler to have started an All-Ireland senior hurling final both as a goalkeeper and as an outfield player (he managed it in the last 30 years)?

1879 Name the Offaly hurler who scored 3-8 against Kilkenny in the 1989 Leinster final?

1880 In either league or championship, name the only captain in history to depart the field with a trophy, despite having lost a national final, and give the reason why?

ANSWERS PAGE 239

CLUB HURLING AND FOOTBALL

1881 Who managed St Vincent's to the 2008 All-Ireland club football title?

1882 Which year in the last 20 years was an All-Ireland club hurling semi-final played in Croke Park along with an All-Ireland club football final on March 17th?

1883 Who are the only divisional side to win an All-Ireland club football title?

1884 John McCarthy captained which side to an All-Ireland club hurling title in the last five years?

1885 Name the last hurler to play in provincial club hurling finals with two different clubs (he managed it in the last five years)?

1886 Who managed Nemo Rangers to the 2008 All-Ireland club final?

1887 Name the three Clare clubs to have contested All-Ireland club hurling finals?

1888 Name the three Derry clubs to have won All-Ireland club football titles?

1889 Who captained Athenry to successive All-Ireland club hurling titles in 2000 and 2001?

1890 Name the only Munster club outside of Cork and Kerry to win an All-Ireland club football title?

ANSWERS PAGE 239

1891 Who were the first Galway club to win an All-Ireland club hurling title?

1892 In which year were the All-Ireland club hurling and football finals all-ticket because the Hogan Stand was demolished?

1893 Who are the only club in the last 20 years to retain their Munster club hurling title?

1894 Name the former Waterford and Cork footballer who captained Nemo Rangers in the 2008 All-Ireland club final?

1895 Name the two managers to manage three All-Ireland club winning teams?

1896 Name the player who won an All-Ireland club hurling medal on the field of play, 21 years after he won an All-Ireland senior hurling medal?

1897 Name the three managers in the last ten years to have managed a team to an All-Ireland club football title after having won an All-Ireland club title with the same club?

1898 The club Oisin contested an All-Ireland club football quarter-final in the last 15 years. From which city did they hail?

1899 Apart from St Finbarr's, name the only other club to contest Munster club hurling and football finals?

1900 Name two of the three players who started All-Ireland club hurling finals in three different decades (they were all with the same club)?

ANSWERS PAGE 239

WEXFORD GENERAL KNOWLEDGE

1901 True or False. George O'Connor played his last game for the county in the 1996 All-Ireland hurling final?

1902 Former Wexford defender Declan Ruth was commonly known by which nickname?

1903 In which year did Good Counsel win their first and only All-Ireland Colleges football title?

1904 Name the coach who trained Good Counsel to that All-Ireland title?

1905 Name the two Wexford hurlers in the top 20 all-time senior hurling championship scorers?

1906 Name the only Wexford player to play in Leinster hurling and football finals in the last 50 years?

1907 Name the Wexford hurler who won a Dublin county hurling medal with Ballyboden St Enda's in 2007?

1908 Before 2008, when was the last time Wexford reached a Leinster senior football final?

1909 Who scored the winning point from a free for Wexford against Dublin in injury time of the 2007 Leinster hurling semi-final?

1910 In which year did Damien Fitzhenry and Rory McCarthy play on a Wexford minor football team that took Meath (who

ANSWERS PAGE 239

went on to win the All-Ireland) to extra-time in a replayed Leinster semi-final?

1911 Name the two Wexford players selected on the GAA's Centenary Hurling Team, comprising players who never won an All-Ireland senior medal?

1912 Who captained Wexford to the 1997 Leinster hurling title?

1913 Name the only Wexford College to win an All-Ireland colleges hurling title?

1914 Name the two Wexford brothers who played (separately) in Leinster senior hurling and football finals in 2008?

1915 Name the Wexford club who achieved the unique feat of winning five Féile na nGael Camogie titles in a row?

1916 Name the two sets of Wexford brothers to have won hurling All-Star awards?

1917 Who managed Wexford to the National League and Leinster hurling finals in 1993?

1918 Seven Wexford men played in six All-Ireland football finals in a row between 1913 and 1918. Name three of them?

1919 Name the two Wexford clubs to have won All-Ireland club ladies' football titles?

1920 Name the only two Wexford hurlers to win All-Ireland senior hurling and football medals?

ANSWERS PAGE 239

HURLERS TURNED REFEREES

1921 True or False? Wexford's Dickie Murphy has refereed more any other referee in hurling history?

1922 Former Galway referee Jimmy Cooney won an All-Ireland senior hurling medal with Galway in which year?

1923 Seanie McMahon, who refereed the classic 2004 Munster hurling final between Cork and Waterford, played in the Munster championship in the 1980s with which county?

1924 Name the former Cork All-Ireland medal winner and GAA President who refereed All-Ireland finals in 1948 and 1950?

1925 Name the former legendary Clare and Dublin goalkeeper who refereed the 1935 All-Ireland final, three years after he had played in the decider for Clare against Kilkenny?

1926 He was on the GAA's Hurling Team of the Millennium and he refereed an All-Ireland semi-final in 1954, just four years after he had played in his last All-Ireland final. Name him?

1927 Name the former Tipperary multiple All-Ireland winner and Munster Council Secretary up until this decade, who was also an inter-county referee?

1928 Jim O'Regan won four All-Ireland medals and had only just finished playing when he refereed the 1936 All-Ireland hurling final. With which county did O'Regan win his medals?

ANSWERS PAGE 240

1929 He was a Clare hurler who won 8 Railway Cup medals and he also refereed Munster hurling finals in 1964 and 1965. Name him?

1930 Ignatius Harney, who won an All-Ireland with Galway, refereed the 1938 All-Ireland final. In which year did Galway win that All-Ireland title, which was their first title (their second didn't arrive until 1980)?

1931 Former Dublin player and inter-county hurling referee, Des Ferguson, was more commonly known by which nickname?

1932 Former Galway hurler and manager, MJ Flaherty, refereed the 1949 All-Ireland final. By which nickname was he more commonly known?

1933 Phil Purcell refereed the 1947 All-Ireland final but he had won an All-Ireland medal in the previous decade with which county?

1934 Tull Considine refereed the 1937 All-Ireland semi-final, just five years after he'd played in the 1932 All-Ireland final with which county?

1935 Jack Mulcahy refereed the 1954 All-Ireland final, just four years after he played in an All-Ireland final with which county?

1936 John Joe Callanan refereed the 1940 All-Ireland but he captained which county to an All-Ireland title ten years earlier in 1930?

1937 The last former inter-county hurler and GAA President to referee at inter-county level was GAA President in the last 25 years. Name him?

1938 Name the former inter-county referee and Dublin hurler, who also managed the Dublin hurlers in the mid 1990s?

1939 Who was the last inter-county hurling referee to play in an All-Ireland hurling final at either club or inter-county level?

1940 Name the Waterford player who had the unique distinction of refereeing the 1945 All-Ireland final, three years before he actually played in the 1948 decider?

ANSWERS PAGE 240

CONTROVERSIAL MANAGERIAL RESIGNATIONS AND UPHEAVALS

1941 Which manager resigned after just one game in the 2008 Munster hurling championship, subsequent to the players issuing a vote of no confidence in him?

1942 Name the manager who was sacked despite reaching an All-Ireland senior football final in the last ten years?

1943 Former Limerick manager Joe McKenna resigned after they were hammered in the 2006 hurling championship by which county?

1944 Name the Cork hurling manager who was forced to step down after the Cork players went on strike in 2002?

1945 Name the Mayo football manager who was forced to resign after the players criticised his methods in 1992?

1946 Name the Limerick manager who resigned after only two games into the 2005 national hurling league?

1947 Name the Dublin manager who stepped down after his side were beaten by Offaly in the league in the autumn of 1997?

1948 Name the Sligo manager who was controversially sacked before a training session in February 2006?

1949 Name the Kilkenny hurling manager who stepped down in the last 15 years, primarily because of the verbal abuse his own brother received from the terraces during a national hurling league semi-final?

ANSWERS PAGE 240

1950 In which year was Tommy Carr sacked as Dublin manager, despite receiving assurances from the county chairman that he would be re-elected?

1951 After John Maughan resigned as Roscommon manager in 2008, name the former Roscommon player who took over as interim manager for two games?

1952 After Sligo were defeated in the 2004 qualifiers by Clare, the Sligo manager refused to train the team for the Tommy Murphy Cup. The decision subsequently cost him his job. Name the manager?

1953 Which hurling manager resigned before the 2008 hurling championship qualifiers, after attendances at training dropped to single figures?

1954 After being appointed to the job in the autumn of 2005, name the Meath manager who got into a big row with the county board over the right to appoint his own selectors (he was replaced as manager after only one season in charge)?

1955 Although Conor Hayes was returned as Galway hurling manager in 2005 (when they reached an All-Ireland final) another manager had been voted in that year but the decision was returned after delegates spoke up about giving Hayes another chance. Name the manager who was denied the job on that occasion?

1956 Name the Dublin hurling manager who stepped down in the middle of the 2005 championship?

ANSWERS PAGE 240

1957 After JJ Barrett was forced to step down as Wexford football manager in 1999 following an altercation with referee Michael Curley after a league game against Cavan, name the selector who took over as manager?

1958 Name the Carlow football manager who stepped down only a few weeks before the 2004 championship?

1959 Name the two hurling managers in the last ten years to step down after leading their team to an All-Ireland final?

1960 When Babs Keating stepped down as Offaly manager in 1998, it was largely in response to a newspaper interview given two days after that year's Leinster final by which Offaly player?

WICKLOW GENERAL KNOWLEDGE

1961 Name the Wicklow player who scored the winning goal in the dying seconds of the 2007 Tommy Murphy Cup final?

1962 How many Leinster minor football finals did Wicklow contest in the 1990s – none, one or two?

1963 Former Leinster, Ireland and British and Irish Lions hooker, Shane Byrne, returned to play football with which club in 2008 after a 17-year absence?

1964 On how many occasions did Wicklow's Colm Byrne win the All-Ireland Poc Fada final?

1965 Which Wicklow club lost the 1995 Leinster final to Éire Óg, Carlow after a replay?

1966 Which club did Baltinglass defeat in the 1990 All-Ireland club football final?

1967 Name the former Wicklow player who stepped down as football manager before the 2006 qualifiers began?

1968 Former GAA President, Jack Boothman, was attached to which club?

1969 Which club did Rathnew defeat in a replay in the 2001 Leinster club final?

1970 Along with Jack Boothman, name the only other GAA President from Wicklow?

ANSWERS PAGE 240

1971 True or False? Wicklow won three Kehoe Cup Cups in a row between 2001-03?

1972 Name the two Wicklow players to have represented Ireland at International Rules?

1973 Apart from Baltinglass, An Tochar and Rathnew, name the other Wicklow club to have reached a Leinster club football final?

1974 Name the former Kilkenny All-Ireland medal winner from the last 25 years who subsequently hurled with Wicklow hurlers?

1975 Name the only Wicklow player selected in 1984 on the GAA Centenary team, comprising players who had never won an All-Ireland?

1976 Name the former Dublin footballer who managed Wicklow in the 1997 football championship?

1977 Name the two Wicklow men who refereed the All-Ireland hurling and football finals in 1963?

1978 Name the former Meath footballer who managed Wicklow to an All-Ireland B title in 1992, but who also on occasions tried to balance his playing career with Meath while still managing Wicklow?

1979 Name the Wicklow referee who took charge of both the All-Ireland hurling and football finals in 1966?

1980 Wicklow hurling manager in 2007 and 2008, John Mitchell, won a Dublin SHC medal with which famous club?

ANSWERS PAGE 240

GENERAL KNOWLEDGE

1981 In the last 15 years, two brothers won provincial minor and senior football medals on the same day as goalkeepers. Name them?

1982 The international boxer Darren O'Neill, who almost qualified for the 2008 Olympics, won an All-Ireland U-21 hurling medal with which county?

1983 In 2008, an overseas college captured a Higher Education Hurling championship for the first time in history when they won the Fergal Maher Cup. Name the college?

1984 Name the only outside manager to manage the Tipperary hurlers?

1985 Name the only two players to win Interprovincial (formerly Railway Cup) medals in hurling and football over the last 25 years (both are still current players)?

1986 Two brothers played against each other in the 2008 senior football championship. Name them and the counties they represented?

1987 In a provincial senior football final played in the last 30 years, there was a point scored before the national anthem was played. Name the game and the teams?

1988 Prior to 2008, two sets of brothers have played (between them) in All-Ireland hurling and football finals in the last ten years. Name them?

ANSWERS PAGE 240

1989 Name the two brothers who played for different counties in the 2008 hurling championship (Liam MacCarthy Cup)?

1990 Name the player who captained two different clubs to county senior hurling titles in Munster in the last 15 years?

1991 Name the player who lost All-Ireland senior hurling and football finals in the last 20 years with two different counties?

1992 Name the only player to win an All-Ireland B Championship medal and to captain his county to an All-Ireland senior title (he achieved them both in the last 15 years)?

1993 Prior to 2008, name the only hurler in the last 15 years to play in All-Ireland club, All-Ireland U-21 and All-Ireland senior finals in the same year?

1994 Name the player who played in the 2007 Interprovincial football semi-final before he had made his senior inter-county championship debut?

1995 Name the only hurler to play in All-Ireland senior hurling finals in the 1970s, 1980s and 1990s?

1996 Name the two brothers to play in provincial club football finals with different clubs (not college teams) in the club championship in the last five years?

1997 In which year did Micheal O Hehir do his last TV commentary on an All-Ireland final?

ANSWERS PAGE 240

1998 Name the only Cork club to provide All-Ireland winning captains in hurling and football?

1999 In the last 25 years, a GAA President (who was in his presidency at that time) had a son who captained his county in an All-Ireland minor final. Name the President and his son?

2000 Who was the first blood sub to be sent off in the championship?

ANSWERS PAGE 240

ANSWERS

GENERAL KNOWLEDGE – page 6
1 Four. **2** Henry Shefflin. **3** Paraic Duffy. **4** Monaghan. **5** Richie Bennis. **6** Sean Kelly. **7** Kerry. **8** Dan Shanahan. **9** Birr and Ballyhale Shamrocks. **10** Sean Boylan. **11** True. **12** Waterford. **13** Munster and Connacht – Interprovincial hurling final. **14** Errigal Ciaran. **15** Thomas Freeman. **16** Canada. **17** Christy Cooney. **18** France. **19** Setanta and Aisake. **20** Colm Cooper (Kerry).

MANAGERIAL ROLL CALL 1 – page 8
21 Two. **22** Two. **23** Vincent Mullins. **24** Westmeath. **25** Galway minors. **26** Declan Ryan. **27** Peter Ford. **28** Brian Canavan and Brian McAlinden. **29** Dublin U-21s. **30** UCD. **31** Limerick and Laois. **32** Charlie Mulgrew. **33** Nicky English (Tipperary 2001). **34** Art McRory and Eugene McKenna. **35** 1997. **36** Colm O'Rourke. **37** Antrim and Laois. **38** Eamonn Ryan. **39** 1991. **40** Pat Nally.

ULSTER FOOTBALL GREATS – page 10
41 Five. **42** 1992. **43** Lavey. **44** Martin McHugh. **45** Two. **46** Anthony Tohill. **47** Ardboe. **48** Joe Lennon. **49** Eugene 'Nudie' Hughes. **50** Sean O'Neill. **51** Queen's University Belfast. **52** 2006. **53** 1952. **54** Two. **55** 1961. **56** Jim McKeever (Derry). **57** St John's. **58** John Joe O'Reilly (Cavan). **59** Jim McCullough. **60** Hughie O'Reilly.

GENERAL KNOWLEDGE – page 13
61 Brian Gavin. **62** Stephen Ireland. **63** Ronan O'Gara. **64** Na Piarsaigh. **65** Eddie Brennan and Henry Shefflin. **66** Meath. **67** Joe Canning. **68** 1986. **69** St Flannan's College, Ennis. **70** Tullaroan. **71** Dunloy Cuchulainns. **72** Crossmaglen Rangers, Ballina Stephenites, Nemo Rangers and St Vincent's. **73** Neville Coughlan. **74** Marc Ó Sé. **75** Dan Shanahan. **76** Derek Lyng and Aidan Fogarty. **77** Anthony Nash. **78** Dunmanway. **79** John Mullane (Munster Interprovincial winners in 2007). **80** Dick Fitzgerald.

ANTRIM GENERAL KNOWLEDGE – page 15
81 Paul Duffin. **82** Terrence McNaughton and Dominic McKinley. **83** CJ McGourty. **84** Cavan. **85** Down. **86** Down and Cavan. **87** Ruairí Óg, Cushendall. **88** O'Donovan Rossa (2004). **89** Brian White and PJ O'Hare. **90** Brian McFall. **91** 1951. **92** Mickey Culbert. **93** One. **94** They were suspended from the provincial competition for one season because of a brawl in the 1997 Ulster final against Lavey. **95** Padraig McNamee and Seamus McFerran. **96** Darren O'Hare. **97** Wolfe Tones and St Joseph's, Doora-Barefield. **98** Gary O'Kane. **99** St John's. **100** Six.

CONTROVERSIES – page 17

101 Teddy Holland. **102** Rule 11. **103** Dublin and Meath. **104** Paddy Russell.
105 Paddy Crozier. **106** John Gardiner (Cork). **107** Ballyboden St Enda's. **108** Thomas
Walsh. **109** Derry. **110** Moorefield. **111** 2004. **112** Offaly. **113** Dublin. **114** Waterford.
115 Frank McGuigan. **116** Stephen Grehan. **117** JJ Barrett. **118** Willie Barrett
(Tipperary). **119** Garda College. **120** The referee only played 33 minutes and 24
seconds in the first-half and Down, who lost by two points, complained afterwards
because they felt they were in the ascendancy at the time.

CLUBCALL 1 – page 20

121 Cork. **122** Kilkenny. **123** Galway. **124** Tipperary. **125** Armagh. **126** Kerry. **127** Cork.
128 Clare. **129** Mayo. **130** Waterford. **131** Dublin. **132** Down. **133** Tyrone. **134** Limerick.
135 Cavan. **136** Offaly. **137** Meath. **138** Longford. **139** Galway. **140** Fermanagh.

NEW, SECONDARY AND NOW DEFUNCT COMPETITIONS – page 21

141 Munster. **142** Tyrone. **143** Leinster. **144** 2006. **145** Dublin. **146** Ulster. **147** Galway.
148 Antrim. **149** Leinster. **150** Clare and Fermanagh. **151** Cork. **152** Mayo and
Roscommon. **153** All-Ireland B Championship. **154** Munster. **155** London. **156** Ardfert.
157 Moycullen. **158** Moyle Rovers (Tipperary). **159** Wembley. **160** The Monaghan Cup.

ARMAGH GENERAL KNOWLEDGE – page 23

161 Mullaghbawn. **162** Clonkill. **163** Jim McCorry. **164** Laois. **165** Ger Reid.
166 Roscommon. **167** Bronagh O'Donnell. **168** True. **169** Cork. **170** 1994.
171 Crossmaglen. **172** Fermanagh. **173** Denis Hollywood. **174** 1995. **175** Errigal Ciaran.
176 Jacqui Clarke and Hayley Boyle. **177** 1988. **178** Errigal Ciaran, Castleblayney
Faughs, Enniskillen Gaels, The Loup and Bellaghy. **179** Patricia McAvoy. **180** It was
the first time they had lost a championship match in the Athletic Grounds in 24 years.

NICKNAMES – page 25

181 Ogie. **182** Brick. **183** The Rock. **184** Redser. **185** Nudie. **186** Spike. **187** Mugsy.
188 Horse. **189** Banty. **190** Inky. **191** Sparrow. **192** Ricey. **193** Beefy. **194** Growler.
195 The Rattler. **196** Fingers. **197** Squires. **198** Fox. **199** Sid. **200** Hub.

TRUE OR FALSE – page 26

201 False. **202** False. **203** True. **204** True. **205** False. **206** True. **207** True. **208** False.
209 True. **210** True. **211** True. **212** False. **213** True. **214** False (Munster also had two
winners – Clare and Tipperary). **215** True. **216** False (they won one in 1896). **217** False
(St Finbarr's from Cork also achieved that feat). **218** True. **219** False. **220** True.

CARLOW GENERAL KNOWLEDGE – page 28

221 Jim Greene. **222** 1999. **223** O'Toole's. **224** Nemo Rangers. **225** Offaly. **226** Cyril
Hughes. **227** 1954 . **228** Knockmore (Mayo) and Mullaghbawn (Armagh). **229** Tommy
Buggy. **230** Daniel St Ledger. **231** St Mary's, Galway. **232** Garvan Ware. **233** Cyril

Hughes. **234** John Byrne. **235** Hughie Brennan. **236** Johnny Nevin and Joe Hayden. **237** Paddy Quirke. **238** True. **239** Liamy Walsh. **240** Peeny Whelan (1945).

ALL-IRELAND FINAL RTÉ MAN OF THE MATCH IN THE LAST 15 YEARS – page 30
241 Eddie Brennan. **242** Aidan O'Mahony. **243** 2004. **244** Michael Donnellan.
245 2003. **246** 1997. **247** Kevin Hughes. **248** Liam Dunne. **249** Tommy Dunne (2001).
250 Nine. **251** Mickey Linden. **252** Ben O'Connor. **253** Brian Corcoran. **254** 1995.
255 Brian Whelahan (Offaly). **256** Colm Cooper (Kerry). **257** 2000. **258** Aidan Fogarty.
259 Johnny McGurk. **260** Padraig Kelly (Galway – 1993).

SENIOR CAMOGIE AND LADIES' FOOTBALL – page 32
CAMOGIE: **261** Stella Synott. **262** Ulster. **263** UCD. **264** 2004. **265** Mary Leacy.
266 Therese O'Callaghan. **267** Kilkenny. **268** True. **269** Gemma O'Connor.
270 Michael Cleary. LADIES' FOOTBALL: **271** Juliete Murphy. **272** Frank Browne.
273 Valerie Mulcahy. **274** Armagh. **275** Cork. **276** Mayo. **277** Monaghan and Cavan.
278 Michael Ryan. **279** The Brendan Martin Cup. **280** Rhona O'Mahony, daughter of
John O'Mahony.

CAVAN GENERAL KNOWLEDGE – page 34
281 Ollie Brady and Dermot McCabe. **282** Jim Smith (1933). **283** Baileboro (1995).
284 1972. **285** Justin McNulty. **286** 1995. **287** PJ Duke. **288** Shannon Gaels.
289 Aaron Donoghue. **290** Brendan. **291** Peter Donohue. **292** Offaly. **293** Peter and
Larry Reilly. **294** 1928. **295** Cork. **296** Charlie Gallagher. **297** Stephen King, Jim Reilly,
Dermot McCabe and Larry Reilly. **298** Four. **299** Cavan Slashers. **300** The 'Babe Ruth'
of Gaelic football.

NAME THE YEAR – page 36
301 2000. **302** 2005. **303** 1998. **304** 2005. **305** 2003. **306** 2005. **307** 1995. **308** 2000.
309 2000. **310** 2001. **311** 2003. **312** 1996. **313** 1989. **314** 1987. **315** 1996. **316** 2001.
317 1992. **318** 2004 . **319** 1989. **320** 1978.

FILL IN THE MISSING PARTS IN THE CLUB NAMES 1 – page 38
321 Stephenites. **322** Ballagh. **323** Rangers. **324** Deel Rovers. **325** Mitchel's.
326 Gaels. **327** McQuillan's. **328** Sarsfields. **329** All-Whites. **330** Shamrocks.
331 Stars. **332** Faughs. **333** McHales. **334** Cuchulainn's. **335** Shamrocks.
336 Shamrocks. **337** Commercials. **338** Harriers. **339** Gaels. **340** Harps.

CLARE GENERAL KNOWLEDGE – page 39
341 Tulla. **342** Kevin Kennedy. **343** 1991. **344** Ennis CBS. **345** Doonseg, Kilmurry-
Ibrickane, St Senan's Kilkee and Kilrush Shamrocks. **346** 2001. **347** 2005. **348** 2005.
349 Aeroflot. **350** 1993. **351** Brian O'Connell. **352** Ballina Stephenites. **353** Donal
Tuohy. **354** Kilrush Shamrocks. **355** Niall Gilligan. **356** Martin Daly and Odran
O'Dwyer. **357** Frank Lohan. **358** Seamus Durack. **359** Two. **360** Paddy Vaughan and
Pat Vaughan.

HARD-LUCK STORIES – page 41

361 JJ Delaney. **362** Erins Isle. **363** Sean Flood. **364** Dermot Deasy. **365** Ja Fallon. **366** Brian O'Meara. **367** Anthony Lynch. **368** 1980. **369** Martin Shovlin. **370** Cappawhite. **371** 1990. **372** Tommy Carr. **373** Nigel Shaughnessy. **374** Adrian Cush. **375** Iggy Clarke. **376** Paul Delaney. **377** 1969. **378** Graham Canty. **379** To facilitate the Pope's arrival in Ireland. **380** Eddie Dowling.

OUTSIDE MANAGERS – page 44

381 Wexford and Carlow. **382** Leitrim and Galway. **383** Jim McKernan. **384** Sligo, Donegal and Mayo. **385** Clare, Fermanagh and Roscommon. **386** Laois. **387** Two. **388** Galway. **389** Padraig Nolan. **390** Cavan. **391** Tom Carr. **392** Offaly. **393** Carlow, Wexford and Offaly. **394** John Tobin. **395** Clare. **396** Wexford. **397** Galway (1979). **398** Clare. **399** Mick Higgins. **400** Eugene McGee (Offaly in 1982) and John O'Mahony (Galway 1998 and 2001).

CORK GENERAL KNOWLEDGE – page 46

401 Tomás Mulcahy. **402** UCC and Castlehaven. **403** 'Hero' and 'Fraggy'. **404** Limerick Institute of Technology. **405** Dave Barry. **406** Teddy McCarthy. **407** Diarmuid O'Donovan, Liam Hodnett, Mick O'Loughlin and Teddy McCarthy. **408** John O'Driscoll. **409** Colin Corkery. **410** Bertie Óg and Tadhg Murphy. **411** Conor Counihan. **412** Long Puck. **413** Ray Cummins, Jimmy Barry-Murphy and Denis Coughlan. **414** Jimmy Barry-Murphy, Christy Ryan, Teddy McCarthy, Denis Walsh and Seán Óg Ó hAilpín. **415** Des Cullinane. **416** Kevin Ger O'Sullivan and Brendan Jer O'Sullivan. **417** Frank Murphy, PJ Murphy, John Meyler Bertie Óg Murphy (manager) and Pat McDonnell. **418** Christy Ring, Charlie McCarthy, Tony O'Sullivan, Joe Deane and Jack Lynch. **419** Teddy O'Brien. **420** Barry Egan and Setanta Ó hAilpín.

FOOTBALL ALL-STARS – page 48

421 Darragh, Tomás and Marc Ó Sé (2007). **422** Kevin McCloy and Paddy Bradley. **423** Karl Lacey. **424** Matty Forde. **425** Kieran McGeeney, Aidan O'Rourke and Enda McNulty. **426** 2003 (all from Kerry, Tyrone and Armagh). **427** Full-back. **428** Mayo. **429** Dermot McCabe. **430** Three. **431** Pat Spillane, Mikey Sheehy, Ger Power and Jack O'Shea. **431** Peter Canavan. **433** True. **434** Martin McHugh. **435** Two. **436** Tony Scullion and Anthony Tohill. **437** Kevin McCabe. **438** Barry Owens, Marty McGrath and Matty Forde. **439** Declan Browne and Matty Forde. **440** Paddy Linden (Monaghan), Gary Walsh (Donegal) and Finbarr McConnell (Tyrone).

HURLING CAPTAINS' PARADE – page 50

441 Damien Reale. **442** Jackie Tyrrell. **443** Michael Walsh. **444** Ollie Canning. **445** 1998. **446** Eoin Kelly and Paul Ormonde. **447** Brian Lohan. **448** Pat Mulcahy. **449** Ger 'Redser' O'Grady. **450** Alan Browne. **451** 2005. **452** True. **453** Paddy Barry (Cork) and Noel Skehan (Kilkenny). **454** Andy and Martin Comerford, Brian and Frank Lohan. **455** 2001. **456** 2003. **457** Charlie Carter. **458** Johnny Pilkington. **459** Bobby Ryan. **460** Henry Shefflin (Ballyhale Shamrocks and Kilkenny in 2007).

DERRY GENERAL KNOWLEDGE – page 52
461 John McCloskey. **462** Offaly. **463** Chris Browne. **464** Kilkenny. **465** Tyrone, Donegal and Meath. **466** True. **467** Errigal Ciaran. **468** Eoin McCloskey. **469** Michael Conlon. **470** Malachy O'Rourke. **471** Danny Quinn. **472** 2001. **473** Gerard O'Kane. **474** Kieran McKeever and Kevin McCloy. **475** Four. **476** Johnny McBride. **477** Kevin McNaughton. **478** Emmett McKeever (Dungiven). **479** Seamus Downey, Kieran McKeever and Brian McGilligan. **480** Sean Marty Lockhart.

PLAYERS WHO CAME OUT OF RETIREMENT OR WHO MADE NOTABLE COMEBACKS – page 54
481 Ollie Canning. **482** Diarmaid Marsden. **483** Fergal Hartley. **484** Brendan Devenney. **485** 2002. **486** 2002 (he announced it that January). **487** Martin Storey. **488** Larry Tompkins. **489** Ja Fallon. **490** Darren Fay. **491** Jimmy Keaveney. **492** Denis Mulcahy. **493** Aidan O'Rourke. **494** Ciaran O'Sullivan. **495** Ronan Gallagher. **496** Eoin Liston. **497** Martin O'Doherty. **498** Mick O'Connell. **499** Dave Creedon. **500** 1974.

GENERAL KNOWLEDGE – page 57
501 1999. **502** Dromard. **503** Down (Down and South Down). **504** Laune Rangers (1996). **505** Ardfinnan. **506** Darragh and Marc O Se. **507** Michael Ryan (Templederry). **508** Tipperary (2002). **509** Galway. **510** Billy O'Shea. **511** Kieran Mulvey. **512** Pat O'Connor. **513** Mayo. **514** Kevin Walsh. **515** 2001. **516** Kerry and Dublin. **517** Kieran McGeeney (Armagh and Kildare) and Jason Ryan (Waterford and Wexford). **518** 1993. **519** Kerry in 2006. **520** Anthony Daly (Clare).

DONEGAL GENERAL KNOWLEDGE – page 59
521 Jimmy McGuinness. **522** Eamonn and Neil McGee. **523** Michael Boyle. **524** PJ McGowan. **525** Four Masters. **526** Jimmy McGuinness and Christy Toye. **527** NUIG (2003). **528** Two. **529** Martin McHugh. **530** Killygordon. **531** St Joseph's. **532** *Donegal Democrat*. **533** 1991. **534** Martin Gavigan. **535** Against Fermanagh in 2000. **536** Patsy McGonagle. **537** Donegal goalkeeper Gary Walsh was adjudged to have stepped over the goal-line after fielding a long ball. Even TV pictures failed to confirm the umpire's decision. **538** Martin McHugh (1993). **539** Wore numbers on their jerseys. **540** Columba McDyer (he played with Cavan in 1947).

FOOTBALL'S EVOLUTION THROUGH THE LAST 65 YEARS – page 61
541 One. **542** Kevin Heffernan. **543** True. **544** Three. **545** Sean Doherty. **546** Pat Spillane. **547** Paudie O'Mahoney. **548** 1977. **549** Twelve. **550** Four. **551** Matt Gallagher. **552** Kerry and Cork. **553** Pat McEnaney. **554** Padraig Joyce. **555** Three. **556** Dessie Ryan.. **557** Fr Gerard McAleer. **558** Ger O'Keeffe. **559** True. **560** Three.

OUTSTANDING HURLERS AND FOOTBALLERS WHO NEVER WON AN ALL-IRELAND SENIOR MEDAL WITH THEIR COUNTY – page 64
561 Mickey Kearns. **562** Sean Stack. **563** Dermot Earley Senior. **564** 1984. **565** Two

(1993 and 1999). **566** Galway. **567** Willie Joe Padden. **568** Kevin Armstrong. **569** Eight. **570** Patrickswell. **571** Glenn Ryan. **572** 1992. **573** 1999. **574** 1986. **575** 1998. **576** Ruairí Óg, Cushendall. **577** Four. **578** Martin McQuillan. **579** Martin. **580** Dinny Allen (Cork).

DOWN GENERAL KNOWLEDGE – page 67

581 Mayo. **582** True (Kilclief). **583** Derry. **584** Martin Bailie. **585** Willie and Liam Doyle. **586** Three. **587** Six. **588** East Kerry. **589** Kevin Mussen, Paddy Doherty, Joe Lennon, Paddy O'Rourke and DJ Kane. **590** Downpatrick. **591** Ger Monan. **592** James Colgan. **593** Ballycran. **594** Liam Doyle. **595** Graham, Liam and Eoin Clarke. **596** Barry Breen. **597** Noel Sands. **598** Ambrose Rodgers senior and Ambrose Rodgers, Ross Carr and Aidan Carr. **599** Cavan. **600** Noel Sands.

FOOTBALL CAPTAINS' PARADE – page 69

601 Derek Kavanagh. **602** Glenn Ryan. **603** Brian Dooher. **604** Kevin McCloy. **605** 2000. **606** Collie Moran. **607** Tomás Quinn. **608** Darragh Ó Sé. **609** Jarlath Burns. **610** Tommy Drumm. **611** Graham Canty. **612** Richie Connor. **613** St Finbarr's (Cork). **614** Brian Ruane. **615** Peter Canavan (Tyrone – 2002, 2003). **616** David O'Shaughnessy. **617** Peter Canavan (Tyrone). **618** Tony Hanahoe (Dublin 1976, 1977). **619** Trevor Giles (Meath – minor in 1993 and senior in 2001). **620** John McEntee (Crossmaglen Rangers 1998 and 2007).

HURLERS WHO HAVE PLAYED IN ALL-IRELAND FINALS OVER THE LAST 20 YEARS – page 71

621 Limerick. **622** Kilkenny. **623** Offaly. **624** Galway. **625** Tipperary. **626** Antrim. **627** Clare. **628** Cork. **629** Offaly. **630** Kilkenny. **631** Galway. **632** Tipperary. **633** Galway. **634** Antrim. **635** Limerick. **636** Galway. **637** Cork. **638** Limerick. **639** Wexford. **640** Clare.

DUBLIN GENERAL KNOWLEDGE – page 72

641 Jim and Brian Stynes. **642** Endn McNulty (Ballyboden St Enda's and Na Fianna). **643** Kevin Fennelly. **644** True. **645** Lar Foley. **646** 2006. **647** Jason Sherlock. **648** Limerick and Cork. **649** Coman Goggins. **650** Mick Bermingham. **651** 1977. **652** Joe Fortune. **653** Tommy Drumm, Robbie Kelleher and Paddy Cullen. **654** Una O'Connor. **655** Keith Barr, Dessie Farrell, Charlie Redmond and Paul Clarke. **656** UCD, St Vincent's, Parnell's, Thomas Davis, Erins Isle, Kilmacud Crokes, Na Fianna and St Brigid's. **657** Joe McNally. **658** Coman Goggins. **659** Noel Drumgoole. **660** Jackie and Pat Gilroy.

GENERAL KNOWLEDGE – page 75

661 Mick Jacob. **662** Sarsfields, Athenry, Clarinbridge, Portumna and Loughrea. **663** Derry. **664** Diarmuid Healy. **665** John Divilly. **666** 1991. **667** Adare. **668** Westmeath. **669** Declan O'Sullivan (Kerry). **670** Sean Og O hAilpin. **671** Brendan

Cummins. **672** Pete Finnerty. **673** Anthony Daly and Eamonn Cregan. **674** 2005.
675 Offaly and Limerick played in the 2003 hurling qualifiers on a Thursday evening
in Thurles. **676** Aghada. **677** Kieran Murphy (Erins Own). **678** Diarmuid O'Sullivan.
679 Meath, Laois, Kerry, Offaly and Dublin. **680** Mark and John Grimley (Armagh).

PLAYERS WHO MADE NOTABLE POSITIONAL SWITCHES – page 78
681 Longford. **682** Ken McGrath. **683** Centre-back. **684** Vincent Corey. **685** Clare.
686 True. **687** Fergal Hartley. **688** John Carroll. **689** Michael Jacob. **690** Bryan Sheehan.
691 True. **692** Pat Fox. **693** Graham Geraghty. **694** 2003. **695** Eugene Coughlan.
696 TJ Ryan. **697** Frank Lohan. **698** Pat Delaney. **699** Dessie Donnelly. **700** John Troy.

FERMANAGH GENERAL KNOWLEDGE – page 81
701 Peter McGinnitty. **702** Niall Tinney. **703** Pat King and his sons Shane and Barry.
704 Terry Ferguson. **705** 1993. **706** 'The Cat'. **707** Three. **708** Ollie McShea. **709** Peter
McGinnity. **710** Liam McBarron. **711** 1996 and 2000. **712** Cork. **713** Cork. **714** Barry
Owens and Shane Goan. **715** Wexford. **716** John and Ciaran McElroy. **717** Patsy Treacy
of 'Treacy Concrete'. **718** Paul Brewster. **719** Peter McGinnitty, Paul Brewster and
Marty McGrath. **720** PT Treacy.

LAST TITLE WON AS A MANAGER – page 83
721 All-Ireland senior title in 2006. **722** Ulster title in 2006. **723** Munster title in 1998.
724 Munster title in 2006. **725** Connacht senior title in 2004. **726** Connacht title in
2003. **727** Munster title in 2006. **728** League title in 1997. **729** League title in 2004.
730 All-Ireland title in 2001. **731** League title in 2000 with Derry. **732** League title in
2000. **733** Munster title in 2000. **734** League title in 1995. **735** Dr McKenna Cup in
1998. **736** All-Ireland title in 1982. **737** Leinster title in 1985. **738** League title in 1989.
739 O'Byrne Cup in 2004. **740** League title in 1994 with Tipperary.

**OUTSTANDING INDIVIDUAL HURLING AND FOOTBALL SCORING
PERFORMANCES OVER THE LAST 30 YEARS** – page 85
741 Limerick. **742** Brian Carroll. **743** Frankie Dolan. **744** Offaly. **745** John Mullane.
746 Steven McDonnell. **747** Paul Flynn (Waterford). **748** Henry Shefflin. **749** 2002.
750 2005. **751** Henry Shefflin (2006). **752** Eugene Cloonan. **753** Eoin Kelly (Tipperary).
754 1980. **755** Denis Byrne. **756** Matty Forde. **757** Oisin McConville. **758** Oliver
Collins. **759** Mick Brennan. **760** Dermot Kelly.

GALWAY GENERAL KNOWLEDGE – page 87
761 Fergal Healy. **762** 1998. **763** St Raphael's. **764** Annette Clarke. **765** Four.
766 Imelda Hobbins. **767** Michael Meehan. **768** John and Joe Connolly, Jimmy and Joe
Cooney. **769** Michael McGrath. **770** Salthill and An Cheathru Rua. **771** Mick Curley.
772 Greg Kennedy. **773** Kieran Comer. **774** Clarinbridge. **775** 1959. **776** Seanie
Duggan and Joe Salmon. **777** Bosco McDermott. **778** John Connolly. **779** Mattie and
Michael Coleman. **780** Niall McInerney and Vincent Mullins.

TRADITIONAL AND NEW RIVALRIES – page 89

781 One. **782** Two – 1994 and 1995. **783** True. **784** Michael Doyle. **785** Jack Sheedy. **786** John Maughan. **787** Neither – both won four and drew one. **788** 2001. **789** Frankie Dolan senior and Dessie Dolan senior. **790** Tony Doran. **791** Frankie Carroll. **792** Fermanagh. **793** 2000-02. **794** Moy. **795** Two. **796** Graiguecullen. **797** Clanrye. **798** Ballinderry. **799** John Denton. **800** Ballydesmond

GENERAL KNOWLEDGE – page 92

801 Seán Óg de Paor. **802** Loughgiel Shamrocks. **803** Andrew McCann. **804** Mayo. **805** 2002. **806** Seamus Hickey (Limerick). **807** Killian Young (Kerry). **808** 2004. **809** Daniel Goulding (Cork). **810** Keith Higgins (Mayo). **811** Loughmore-Castleleiney. **812** Seamus Callinan and John O'Brien. **813** Jack O'Shea, Barney Rock and David Beggy. **814** 1992. **815** Tony Browne and Dan Shanahan. **816** Paddy Buggy. **817** Four. **818** John Egan. **819** Brian Whelahan (Birr in 1991 and 2007). **820** Eddie Keher (Kilkenny).

KERRY GENERAL KNOWLEDGE – page 94

821 Ger Power. **822** Pat O'Shea (Kerry), Tomás Ó Flaharta (Westmeath) and John Evans (Tipperary). **823** Paul Galvin. **824** Denis 'Ogie' Moran. **825** Derry and John O'Shea. **826** 2002. **827** 1999. **828** True. **829** Donncha Walsh. **830** True. **831** Sean and Tommy Walsh, Denis 'Ogie' and David Moran, John and Eoin Kennedy. **832** Tom Collins. **833** Kilmoyley. **834** John O'Keeffe. **835** Brendan Lynch 1-7 v Offaly in 1972 (drawn game). **836** True. **837** Nine. **838** 1980. **839** Gary McMahon. **840** Kieran Kennedy (he won with St Flannan's College in 1991).

GREAT SERVANTS OF THE LAST 20 YEARS – page 96

841 Anthony Rainbow. **842** Seamus Moynihan. **843** 60. **844** Tony Browne. **845** Mickey Linden. **846** John Quane. **847** Liam Dunne. **848** Mark Foley. **849** 1994. **850** Paul McGrane. **851** Pat Spillane. **852** Paul Flynn. **853** James Nallen. **854** Joe Cooney. **855** Joe Dooley. **856** Johnny Nevin. **857** Frank Lohan. **858** John Cooper. **859** Stephen Melia. **860** Gary Savage.

YOUNG STARS – page 98

861 1996. **862** Andrew O'Shaughnessy. **863** True. **864** National League title. **865** Richie Murray. **866** Donie Brennan. **867** John Reddan. **868** Three. **869** Paul Conroy. **870** Stephen O'Brien. **871** 2004. **872** 1987. **873** 1973. **874** 1996. **875** Diarmaid Marsden. **876** Cathal Naughton. **877** Brian Corcoran. **878** Michael Murphy. **879** 1958. **880** Joe Canning (Galway).

KILDARE GENERAL KNOWLEDGE – page 101

881 1991. **882** 1993. **883** Down. **884** Andrew McLoughlin. **885** 2004. **886** Mick Monahan. **887** Ollie Crinnigan (1978). **888** Ben Dorney. **889** Gary Whyte. **890** St Brigid's (Dublin). **891** Martin Lynch. **892** Clane. **893** Raheens and Moorefield. **894** Paudie Reidy and David Harney. **895** Two. **896** Willie McCreery. **897** Paul McCormack. **898** John Wyse Power (1884-87). **899** He was the first player to lift the

Sam Maguire, the year it first went up for competition. **900** Frank Burke (he won both medals with Dublin).

FITZGIBBON AND SIGERSON CUPS – page 103
901 University of Ulster, Jordanstown. **902** Waterford Institute of Technology. **903** Dublin City University. **904** Tipperary. **905** Eamonn Corcoran. **906** Ken Coogan. **907** IT Tralee. **908** University of Ulster Jordanstown. **909** IT Tralee (although they won their first title in 1997 under the name of Tralee RTC). **910** Waterford IT. **911** University College Cork (UCC). **912** Stephen Lucey. **913** University of Limerick. **914** Kevin Moran. **915** Galway Mayo Institute of Technology (GMIT) and Dublin Institute of Technology (DIT). **916** John Lee. **917** Eoin and TJ Reid. **918** Jimmy McGuinness from Donegal (with ITT and UUJ). **919** Brendan, Dara and Oisin Ó hAnnaidh (Wicklow). **920** Queens University Belfast.

GENERAL KNOWLEDGE – page 105
921 Killian Young. **922** Kevin Hynes. **923** Michael 'Babs' Keating. **924** False (They beat them in the 1977 All-Ireland U-21 final). **925** Andy Comerford (Kildare – former Kilkenny winning captain from 2002). **926** Brendan Maher. **927** True. **928** David Clarke (Mayo and Ballina Stephenites). **929** Richie Power and Richie Power junior. **930** Graham Clarke (Down). **931** Three. **932** Fingal. **933** 1977. **934** Ian Dowling. **935** Damien Fox (Laois manager who played for Tullamore). **936** 1985 – Offaly v Antrim. **937** Pat Fox, Cormac Bonnar and Nicky English. **938** Frank and Alan Cummins. **939** Ger Fitzgerald, Kevin Hennessy and John Fitzgibbon. **940** Carlow, Longford and Louth.

KILKENNY GENERAL KNOWLEDGE – page 108
941 1991. **942** Fenians, James Stephens, Ballyhale Shamrocks, St Martin's, Glenmore, Graigue-Ballycallan and O'Loughlin Gaels. **943** 1993. **944** Two. **945** 1988. **946** London. **947** Frank Cummins. **948** 1997. **949** John Hoyne. **950** Gorta. **951** Tom 'Cloney' Brennan. **952** True. **953** Jack and Pierce Grace. **954** Eddie Keher, Pat Henderson, Noel Skehan and Frank Cummins. **955** Pierce Grace. **956** James Nowlan. **957** Andy and Martin Comerford, Tom and Noel Hickey, Jimmy and Ken Coogan, Richie and Paddy Mullally. **958** James McDermott (1990 minor team) and DJ Carey (2003 seniors). **959** Cork. **960** Dick, Eddie and Mick Doyle.

ALL-IRELAND SENIOR HURLING FINALS FROM THE LAST 20 YEARS – page 110
961 Waterford. **962** Seven. **963** Anthony Daly (Clare). **964** Davy Fitzgerald, Brian Lohan, Frank Lohan, Sean McMahon and Jamesie O'Connor. **965** Henry Shefflin. **966** Ollie Canning, Fergal Healy, David Tierney, Alan Kerins, Derek Hardiman and Richie Murray. **967** Pat Mulcahy. **968** Pat O'Connor. **969** False (Kilkenny and Offaly contested All-Ireland finals in 1998 and 2000). **970** Johnny Pilkington. **971** John Fitzgibbon, Mark Foley, Kevin Hennessy and Tomás Mulcahy. **972** DJ Carey, John Power and Willie O'Connor. **973** Tipperary (between 1949-52). **974** Dublin. **975** Eddie and Willie O'Connor, Andy and Martin Comerford. **976** Colm Bonnar, Conal Bonnar,

John Leahy, Declan Ryan and Noel Sheehy. **977** Terence and Brian Murray (Limerick). **978** DJ Carey. **979** Gerry and Diarmuid Kirwan (Offaly and Cork). **980** Nicky English (Tipperary), John Fitzgibbon (Cork), Damien Quigley (Limerick), DJ Carey (Kilkenny) and Mark O'Leary (Tipperary).

FILL IN THE MISSING PARTS IN THE CLUB NAMES 2 – page 112
981 Crokes. **982** St Joseph's. **983** St Mary's. **984** MacDonaghs. **985** St Mary's. **986** Rovers. **987** St Mary's. **988** Kevin Lynch's. **989** St Canice's. **990** Kickhams. **991** Borris. **992** St Eunan's. **993** Cormacs. **994** Gaels. **995** Naomh Eoin. **996** Drombane. **997** Moylough. **998** Shamrocks. **999** Emmett's. **1000** Cuchulainn's.

LAOIS GENERAL KNOWLEDGE – page 113
1001 Colm Parkinson. **1002** 1996. **1003** Gabriel Lawlor. **1004** James Young. **1005** Portlaoise, St Joseph's and Ballyroan. **1006** Paudie Butler and Dinny Cahill. **1007** Colm Browne. **1008** Declan, Mark and Darren Rooney. **1009** Robert O'Keeffe. **1010** 2001. **1011** 2007. **1012** Colm Browne. **1013** Jack, Bill, Chris and Mick Delaney. **1014** Kieran Kelly. **1015** Paul Cuddy. **1016** John Lyons. **1017** Tony McMahon. **1018** John Walsh. **1019** Christy O'Brien. **1020** Pat Dunphy.

GAA POLITICIANS – page 115
1021 John O'Mahony. **1022** Jimmy Deenihan. **1023** Tony Dempsey. **1024** Dublin. **1025** John O'Leary (Dublin) and Graham Geraghty (Meath). **1026** John Wilson. **1027** True. **1028** John Donnellan. **1029** Roscommon. **1030** Sean Flanagan. **1031** Austin Stack. **1032** Des Foley. **1033** Kerry. **1034** Big Tom. **1035** Mick and John Donnellan (Galway). **1036** Henry Kenny. **1037** Dan Spring. **1038** Kevin Fennelly (Kilkenny). **1039** John F Bailey. **1040** Brendan Corish.

ODD ONE OUT – page 118
1041 Castlebar Mitchells – the other two Mayo clubs have won All-Irelands. **1042** Cork IT – they have never won a Fitzgibbon Cup title while the other two have. **1043** Martin Comerford – he plays for O'Loughlin Gaels while the other two play for Ballyhale Shamrocks. **1044** Markievicz Park – the other two GAA grounds are in Leinster. **1045** Dungiven – the other two have won All-Ireland club titles. **1046** Con Murphy – he was from Cork but the other two GAA Presidents were from Kilkenny. **1047** Patrickswell – the club is in Limerick while the other two are in Clare. **1048** DIT – they have never won the Sigerson while the other two colleges have. **1049** John McIntyre – he has never managed the Galway hurlers while the other two have. **1050** David Brady – he plays for Ballina Stephenites while the other two play for Crossmolina. **1051** Pat Mullaney – he is a hurling goalkeeper while the other two are football 'keepers. **1052** John Maughan – he has never managed a team to an All-Ireland title while the other two have. **1053** Trevor Giles – he didn't captain Meath to an All-Ireland title while the other two did. **1054** O'Duffy Cup – it's an All-Ireland camogie trophy while the other two are provincial hurling and football cups.

1055 An Ghaeltacht – the other two clubs won All-Ireland club titles. **1056** Diarmuid O'Sullivan – he hasn't captained Cork to an All-Ireland title while the other two have. **1057** Dr Mick Loftus – he wasn't an Ard Stiúrthóir while the other two were. **1058** Toomevara – they have never won an All-Ireland club title while the other two have. **1059** James McCartan – he never captained a team to an All-Ireland senior title while the other two have. **1060** Thurles CBS – they have never won an All-Ireland Colleges title while the other two have.

LEITRIM GENERAL KNOWLEDGE – page 119
1061 Joe Reynolds. **1062** Louth. **1063** Sean O Heslins, Aughawillan, St Mary's and Allen Gaels. **1064** PJ Carroll. **1065** Pakie McGarty. **1066** Johnny Goldrick. **1067** 1990. **1068** Seamus Bonner. **1069** Wexford. **1070** Anne-Marie Cox. **1071** Gareth Phelan. **1072** 1997. **1073** Micky Martin and Séamus Quinn. **1074** St Mary's, Carrick-on-Shannon. **1075** Tom Gannon. **1076** Kildare in Mick O'Dwyer's first competitive match with the county. **1077** Harry O'Carroll (1969). **1078** Tuam. **1079** Niall Finnegan. **1080** St Mary's, Kiltubrid and Feenagh.

MATCH THE FOOTBALLER TO HIS CLUB – page 121
1081 St Oliver Plunkett's/Eoghan Ruadh. **1082** Finuge. **1083** Bantry Blues. **1084** Caltra. **1085** Crossmaglen Rangers. **1086** St Joseph's. **1087** Carrickmore. **1088** Tyrvellspass. **1089** Rhode. **1090** Ballina Stephenites. **1091** Sarsfields. **1092** Magheracloone. **1093** Liatroim. **1094** Enniskillen Gaels. **1095** Gaoth Dobhair. **1096** St Brigid's. **1097** Rathnew. **1098** Bellaghy. **1099** St Anne's. **1100** Cavan Gaels.

FOOTBALL GENERAL KNOWLEDGE – page 122
1101 Tony Scullion. **1102** Tommy Howard. **1103** Na Fianna (Dublin). **1104** Liam Sammon. **1105** Tomás Ó Sé. **1106** Wexford. **1107** Dessie Dolan Senior (Leitrim manager), Dessie and Gary Dolan (with Westmeath). **1108** Ronan Gallagher. **1109** Arles-Kilcruise and Arles-Killeen. **1110** 1980. **1111** Páirc Uí Chaoimh (1984) and Pearse Stadium (2006). **1112** Aidan, Cathal and Marty O'Rourke. **1113** John Gough (Antrim). **1114** Sean Geaney. **1115** Laois. **1116** Johnny Geraghty. **1117** Glenflesk (Kerry) in 2000. **1118** Martin Furlong (Offaly). **1119** Brian McIver had his son Paul with Donegal. **1120** Niall Cahalane (Cork).

LIMERICK GENERAL KNOWLEDGE – page 124
1121 Dave Keane. **1122** Kerry. **1123** Brian Geary. **1124** Westmeath. **1125** Donnacha Sheehan. **1126** Ballybrown, Patrickswell and Kilmallock. **1127** Stephen Lavin. **1128** Albert Shanahan and John Cahill. **1129** John Quane (1999). **1130** Joe O'Connor. **1131** 2005. **1132** Tom McGlinchey. **1133** 1985. **1134** Bangers. **1135** Gary Kirby, Eamonn Cregan and Mick Mackey. **1136** John O'Keeffe. **1137** Gus Ryan. **1138** Paddy Mulvihill. **1139** Eamon Cregan. **1140** Paddy Barrett.

CROKE PARK – A HISTORY – page 126
1141 Frank Dineen. **1142** 1920. **1143** Three. **1144** A Rodeo. **1145** Tipperary. **1146** 1938.

1147 1950. **1148** Pat Nally. **1149** 1959. **1150** Down and Offaly. **1151** 1962. **1152** The 1916 Rising. **1153** 1973. **1154** 1984. **1155** U2. **1156** 1988. **1157** 1993. **1158** 1999. **1159** Special Olympics. **1160** Dublin and Tyrone.

UNLUCKY AND UNFORTUNATE INCIDENTS – page 128
1161 Dessie Dolan. **1162** Tony Browne. **1163** Daithí Regan. **1164** Mickey McQuillan. **1165** Ray Cosgrove. **1166** John Madden. **1167** John Fenton. **1168** Seamus Shinnors. **1169** Ger Power. **1170** Galway. **1171** Mark O'Leary. **1172** Mick O'Connell. **1173** Michael 'Hopper' McGrath. **1174** Mark Ward. **1175** Liam Burke. **1176** Brian Stynes. **1177** John O'Sullivan. **1178** Plunkett Donaghy. **1179** Leonard Enright. **1180** Brian Campion.

LONGFORD GENERAL KNOWLEDGE – page 132
1181 Kenagh. **1182** Kerry. **1183** Paul Barden. **1184** Laois. **1185** Westmeath. **1186** Albert Fallon. **1187** Kilmacud Crokes. **1188** Gareth Ghee. **1189** Three. **1190** Enda Williams. **1191** Four. **1192** Colmcille. **1193** Eamonn Coleman. **1194** True. **1195** Enda, Paul and David Barden. **1196** Michael McCormack. **1197** Matty McLoughlin. **1198** Dessie Dolan. **1199** Dessie Barry and Paul Barden and Liam Tierney. **1200** St Pat's Navan.

GENERAL KNOWLEDGE – page 134
1201 IT Carlow. **1202** Cork IT. **1203** True. **1204** Jack O'Shea (Kerry). **1205** 60 minutes. **1206** Offaly, Galway and Cork. **1207** Liam O'Neill (Laois), Christy Cooney (Cork) and Sean Fogarty (Tipperary). **1208** Westmeath, Carlow and Longford. **1209** Jim English. **1210** Hugh Coughlan. **1211** True. **1212** Paul Grimley. **1213** Denis Byrne. **1214** Diarmuid Healy. **1215** Kevin McCloy (Derry). **1216** Ballycastle McQuillan's (1980). **1217** Sligo. **1218** Dunloy Cuchulainns, O'Donovan Rossa, Ballycastle McQuillans and Loughgiel Shamrocks. **1219** Brian and Aaron Whelahan (with Birr in 2007). **1220** Joe Dooley (Offaly) and Johnny Dooley (Westmeath).

MANAGERIAL ROLL CALL 2 – page 136
1221 Paddy Crozier. **1222** Liam Sheedy. **1223** Brian McGilligan. **1224** Mike McNamara (Offaly and Clare) and Babs Keating (Offaly and Tipperary). **1225** Peter McDonnell. **1226** Jimmy Heaverin. **1227** Four. **1228** Eamonn and Gary Coleman, Mickey and Conleth Moran. **1229** Conor Counihan. **1230** Fr Harry Bohan. **1231** Meath. **1232** Gerald McCarthy (Waterford and Cork). **1233** Pat O'Shea (Dr Crokes and Kerry in 2007). **1234** Offaly. **1235** Westmeath. **1236** Justin McCarthy. **1237** Liam Sammon (Galway). **1238** Mickey Ned O'Sullivan. **1239** Gerry McInerney. **1240** Justin McCarthy.

LOUTH GENERAL KNOWLEDGE – page 138
1241 Drogheda. **1242** Cooley Kickhams. **1243** St Bride's and Knockbridge. **1244** 1997. **1245** Donegal. **1246** Paul and Shane Callan (Paul was a player/selector). **1247** 2002. **1248** Cooley Kickhams and Mattock Rangers. **1249** Paddy Clarke. **1250** Eddie Boyle. **1251** Paddy Keenan (2007). **1252** 2003. **1253** Monaghan. **1254** Kerry. **1255** Kevin Behan. **1256** John Donaldson. **1257** True. **1258** Dundalk Young Irelands. **1259** Gerry Farrell. **1260** The Boyne cable bridge.

MAJOR GAA GROUNDS – page 140

1261 Tom Semple. **1262** 1976. **1263** Brewster Park, Enniskillen. **1264** Pearse Stadium, Galway. **1265** Dick Fitzgerald. **1266** Walsh Park. **1267** Dr Douglas Hyde. **1268** Kingspan Breffni Park, Cavan. **1269** Páirc Tailteann. **1270** Castlebar Mitchels. **1271** O'Moore Park, Portlaoise. **1272** Gaelic Park, New York. **1273** St Brendan's Park. **1274** The Marshes. **1275** Corrigan Park. **1276** Flower Lodge Stadium. **1277** 1993. **1278** 1988. **1279** The John Vesey Stand. **1280** St Jarlath's Park.

INDIVIDUAL TOP SCORERS IN ALL-IRELAND HURLING FINALS OVER THE LAST 35 YEARS – page 142

1281 Eddie Brennan (Kilkenny). **1282** Henry Shefflin. **1283** 2000. **1284** Ben O'Connor. **1285** Martin Comerford. **1286** Jamesie O'Connor. **1287** Four (although he was joint top scorer in 2004 with Joe Deane). **1288** Brian Whelahan. **1289** Ger Fennelly. **1290** PJ Delaney. **1291** Three (although he was joint top scorer with Michael Cleary in 1991). **1292** John Fenton and Kevin Hennessy. **1293** PJ Molloy. **1294** Eamonn Cregan. **1295** 1982. **1296** Pat Moylan. **1297** Richie Bennis. **1298** John Fenton and Seanie O'Leary. **1299** Richie Bennis (Limerick), Eddie Keher (Kilkenny), Pat Moylan (Cork) and Billy Fitzpatrick (Kilkenny). **1300** Nicky English (1988), Joe Cooney (1990) and Eugene Cloonan (2001).

MAYO GENERAL KNOWLEDGE – page 144

1301 John Healy. **1302** Finbar Egan and Jonathan Mullen. **1303** Alan Dillon. **1304** Kenny Golden. **1305** John Casey. **1306** Maurice Sheridan and Gordon Morley. **1307** Ten. **1308** Billy Fitzpatrick. **1309** Willie Casey and Willie McGee. **1310** PJ Loftus. **1311** Three. **1312** 2006. **1313** Padraig Brogan. **1314** 1983. **1315** Ballyhaunis. **1316** Marie Staunton. **1317** Mattie Murphy (Galway). **1318** Keith Higgins, Derek Walsh and Stephen Coyne. **1319** TJ Kilgallon. **1320** Dave Synnott.

ALL-IRELAND FOOTBALL FINALS FROM THE LAST 20 YEARS – page 146

1321 Daniel Goulding. **1322** Three. **1323** Three – Galway, Tyrone and Kerry. **1324** Dinny Allen (Cork). **1325** Charlie Redmond (Dublin). **1326** 1990 and 1992. **1327** Ray Dempsey. **1328** Diarmaio Marsden (Armagh – 2003). **1329** Peter Canavan and Chris Lawn. **1330** Seán Óg Ó hAilpín (Cork – 1999). **1331** Seamus Downey. **1332** Mick Lyons. **1333** Declan Meehan (Galway – replay in 2000) and Tomas O Se (Kerry – 2005). **1334** Neil Collins (Down – 1994), Kevin O'Dwyer (Cork – 1999) and Declan O'Keeffe (Kerry – 2002). **1335** John O'Leary (Dublin), Noel Connelly (Mayo), Kieran McGeeney (Armagh) and Declan O'Sullivan (Kerry). **1336** Anthony Finnerty. **1337** Daragh Ó Sé and Mike Frank Russell. **1338** Colm O'Neill. **1339** Liam Hayes and Tommy Dowd (both Meath). **1340** Noel Connelly (Mayo – 1996), Philip Clifford (Cork – 1989).

COUNTY ANTHEMS AND SONGS – page 148

1341 The Green Glens Of Antrim. **1342** The Boys From The County Armagh. **1343** The Banks Of My Own Lovely Lee. **1344** Mary From Dungloe. **1345** The Star Of The County

Down. **1346** Molly Malone. **1347** Galway Bay. **1348** Rose Of Tralee. **1349** The Curragh Of Kildare. **1350** The Rose Of Mooncoin. **1351** Lovely Laois. **1352** Lovely Leitrim. **1353** Limerick, You're A Lady. **1354** The Boys From The County Mayo. **1355** Beautiful Meath. **1356** The Offaly Rover. **1357** Slievenamon. **1358** The Mountains of Pomeroy. **1359** Boolavogue. **1360** The Meeting Of The Waters.

MEATH GENERAL KNOWLEDGE – page 149

1361 Seneschalstown. **1362** Fergus McMahon. **1363** Ten. **1364** Nigel Nestor. **1365** Eoin Brislane. **1366** Kerry. **1367** Nicky Horan. **1368** Graham Geraghty, Darren Fay and Mark O'Reilly. **1369** Pat Reynolds (1971). **1370** 2002. **1371** Three. **1372** Cavan (2005 qualifiers). **1373** Seneschalstown, Skryne, Summerhill, Walterstown and Dunshaughlin. **1374** Martin O'Connell and Tommy Dowd. **1375** Franciscan College, Gormanstown. **1376** Pat Potterton (1993). **1377** Liam Hayes. **1378** Peter Sullivan. **1379** Mick Cole. **1380** Robbie O'Malley.

SOME OF HURLING'S GREAT PLAYERS FROM THE LAST 30 YEARS – page 151

1381 Two. **1382** Pat Delaney. **1383** 1986. **1384** Six. **1385** 1997. **1386** South Liberties. **1387** 2003. **1388** Nicky English. **1389** Three. **1390** 1992, 2000 and 2002. **1391** 1989. **1392** Éire Óg Annacarty. **1393** Charlie McCarthy. **1394** Blackrock (although he did play with Cobh for one season). **1395** Klute. **1396** Seir Kieran. **1397** Eanna Ryan. **1398** Brian Corcoran (1992). **1399** Johnny Callinan. **1400** An Oireachtas medal.

GENERAL KNOWLEDGE – page 153

1401 Eoin Brosnan. **1402** Ollie Moran. **1403** Ken McGrath. **1404** Tipperary (hurling 1887, football 1889). **1405** Pillar. **1406** Armagh, Ballyhaunis, Limerick and Portlaoise. **1407** False (Tipperary have reached six, Cork have reached five). **1408** Paddy O'Rourke (Down – 1991). **1409** *Gaelic Weekly*. **1410** Johnny Cullotty (Kerry – 1969), Billy Morgan (Cork – 1973) and John O'Leary (Dublin – 1995). **1411** 1981 and 1982. **1412** Seven (Kildare, Dublin, Westmeath, Offaly, Meath, Wexford and Laois). **1413** Kerry. **1414** Kilmaley and Lissy casey. **1415** Antrim, Kilkenny, Louth and Waterford. **1416** Peter Canavan (11 points v Dublin in 1995). **1417** Eddie Keher (2-11 v Tipperary in 1971). **1418** Eamonn Taaffe (Clare – 1995). **1419** John Joyce. **1420** Johnny Kavanagh (Carlow – 1999).

MONAGHAN GENERAL KNOWLEDGE – page 156

1421 Damien Freeman. **1422** Scotstown. **1423** Eamonn McEnaney. **1424** Armagh. **1425** Kerry. **1426** Eugene 'Nudie' Hughes. **1427** Clontibret. **1428** Castleblayney Faughs. **1429** 2001. **1430** Four. **1431** Meath. **1432** Seamus Murray. **1433** 1994. **1434** Joe Hayes. **1435** Michael Slowey. **1436** Michael Greaney. **1437** Hugo Clerkin. **1438** 1939. **1439** 1914 and 1915. **1440** 1992.

A HURLING HISTORY – page 158

1441 Thurles and Meelick. **1442** Tubberadora. **1443** Limerick. **1444** Clare. **1445** Cork. **1446** Cork and Kilkenny. **1447** Two. **1448** Sean Condon. **1449** Two. **1450** Four.

1451 Kilkenny. **1452** Hell's Kitchen. **1453** Five. **1454** True. **1455** Canon Bertie Troy.
1456 Cyril Farrell. **1457** Padraig Horan. **1458** 81. **1459** Sean Flood, son of Tim. **1460** 1999.

FOOTBALL GOALSCORERS OVER THE LAST 35 YEARS – page 161

1461 Jimmy Keaveney. **1462** Oisin McConville. **1463** Eoin Liston (1978). **1464** Michael
Meehan (Galway). **1465** Graham Geraghty. **1466** Jason Reilly. **1467** Paddy Bradley.
1468 Matty Forde (Wexford). **1469** Ger Houlahon. **1470** Mike Frank Russell. **1471**
Benny Coulter. **1472** Ollie Murphy. **1473** Matt Connor. **1474** Eoin Brosnan. **1475** Mikey
Sheehy. **1476** Steven McDonnell (Armagh). **1477** Barney Rock (Dublin). **1478** John
Egan. **1479** Peter Canavan (Tyrone). **1480** Jimmy Barry Murphy.

OFFALY GENERAL KNOWLEDGE – page 164

1481 PJ Ward. **1482** Diarmuid Horan (son of Padraig). **1483** Gerry Fahy. **1484** Brian
Whelahan and Joe Errity. **1485** St Kieran's, Kilkenny. **1486** Carrig-Riverstown.
1487 Nicholas Clavin, Eugene Mulligan, Willie Bryan and Tony McTague. **1488** Pat
O'Connor, Joe and Johnny Dooley. **1489** Johnny Dooley. **1490** True (1988-90).
1491 Michael Hogan. **1492** Ken Casey. **1493** Ballyhale Shamrocks. **1494** Cathal Daly.
1495 Galway. **1496** Johnny Pilkington, Michael Duignan, Joe Dooley and Brian
Whelehan. **1497** Eugene Coughlan. **1498** 1972. **1499** Mick Kennedy. **1500** Finbar
Cullen and Sean Grennan.

CLUBCALL 2 – page 167

1501 Tipperary. **1502** Galway. **1503** Cork. **1504** Limerick. **1505** Westmeath.
1506 Tyrone. **1507** Clare. **1508** Waterford. **1509** Kerry. **1510** Offaly. **1511** Kildare.
1512 Meath. **1513** Dublin. **1514** Laois. **1515** Fermanagh. **1516** Longford. **1517** Wexford.
1518 Mayo. **1519** Armagh. **1520** Louth.

GENERAL KNOWLEDGE – page 168

1521 Jimmy Barry-Murphy, Ray Cummins, Brian Murphy (all Cork) and Liam Currams
(Offaly). **1522** The sin bin. **1523** Wexford, Dublin and Offaly. **1524** Antrim. **1525** PJ
McGrath (Mayo) and Seamus Aldridge (Kildare). **1526** Sean and Tommy Walsh, Denis
'Ogie' Moran and David Moran. **1527** All nine counties competed in the championship
for the first time. **1528** Armagh, Dublin and Galway. **1529** Tommy Doyle (Kerry –
1986). **1530** Charlie McCarthy (Cork – 1978). **1531** Michael Kavanagh. **1532** Sean
McMahon (Clare). **1533** St Brigid's. **1534** Athlone CC. **1535** Ballymacarbery. **1536** False
– it has never been managed. **1537** Mike Frank Russell. **1538** Dudley and Brian Farrell.
1539 UCC (1999). **1540** Longford, Kilkenny and Wexford.

ROSCOMMON GENERAL KNOWLEDGE – page 170

1541 Michael Ryan. **1542** Enon Gavin. **1543** Val Daly. **1544** Mervyn Connaughton.
1545 True. **1546** Mark O'Carroll. **1547** Francie Grehan. **1548** UCD. **1549** Dermot and
Paul Earley. **1550** Kerry. **1551** Abbeyknockmoy. **1552** Donie Shine. **1553** Five.
1554 Gerry O'Malley. **1555** Gerry Fallon. **1556** Aidan Brady and Gerry O'Malley.
1557 Gerry Fallon. **1558**.Mayo. **1559** 1966. **1560** Martin McDermott.

TOP TEN NUMBER OF SENIOR HURLING CHAMPIONSHP APPEARANCES BY SETS OF BROTHERS, PLUS THE TOP TEN HIGHEST SCORING SIBLINGS IN CHAMPIONSHIP HISTORY – page 172

1561 Joe, Johnny and Billy Dooley (Offaly). **1562** Joe, Johnny and Billy Dooley. **1563** Eoin and Paul Kelly. **1564** Pat Henderson. **1565** Billy Rackard. **1566** Jimmy Rackard. **1567** Mick and John Mackey. **1568** Brian, Barry and Simon Whelahan. **1569** Mark and Paddy Corrigan. **1570** Two-Ger and Liam. **1571** Gerry Connolly. **1572** Jim Quigley. **1573** Dan, John, Martin and Pat Quigley (Wexford). **1574** Brian and Frank Lohan. **1575** Tony and Colm Doran. **1576** Tipperary. **1577** Sean. **1578** Dick, Eddie and Mick. **1579** Tommy and Benny Dunne. **1580** John and Mick Mackey.

FOOTBALLERS WHO HAVE PLAYED IN ALL-IRELAND FINALS OVER THE LAST 20 YEARS – page 175

1581 Cork. **1582** Tyrone. **1583** Kerry. **1584** Kerry. **1585** Kildare. **1586** Donegal. **1587** Cork. **1588** Meath. **1589** Derry. **1590** Mayo. **1591** Mayo. **1592** Dublin. **1593** Down. **1594** Galway. **1595** Meath. **1596** Tyrone. **1597** Donegal. **1598** Cork. **1599** Mayo. **1600** Kerry.

SLIGO GENERAL KNOWLEDGE – page 176

1601 Louth. **1602** True. **1603** St Mary's. **1604** Eamonn O'Hara. **1605** Mickey Kearns. **1606** Tubbercurry. **1607** Kieran Quinn. **1608** False. **1609** Paul Durcan. **1610** Desszie Sloyan. **1611** Calry-St Joseph's. **1612** Damien Burke. **1613** Frank Burke. **1614** Mickey Kearins, Barnes Murphy and Eamonn O'Hara. **1615** Clann na nGael. **1616** Tipperary. **1617** They had been nominated to represent Connacht in the All-Ireland semi-final but subsequent to that, Galway defeated them in a Connacht final replay. **1618** Denis Kearney. **1619** Paudie Fitzmaurice. **1620** Mattie Hoey.

MOST PROLIFIC HURLING GOALSCORING SEQUENCES AND LEADING HURLING GOALSCORERS IN ALL-IRELAND SENIOR FINALS BETWEEN 1930-2007 – page 178

1621 Nicky Rackard (Wexford). **1622** Cork. **1623** Dave Clohessy. **1624** Paddy Molloy. **1625** Tony Doran. **1626** Paddy Lalor. **1627** 11. **1628** 1955. **1629** Four. **1630** Seanie O'Leary. **1631** Eddie Keher. **1632** Four. **1633** 1956. **1634** Joe McKenna. **1635** Sean McLoughlin. **1636** Cork. **1637** Dan Shanahan. **1638** Seanie O'Leary. **1639** Seven. **1640** Eddie O'Brien (Cork) 3-1 v Wexford in 1970.

MATCH THE HURLER TO HIS CLUB – page 180

1641 Wolfe Tones. **1642** Oulart-the-Ballagh. **1643** Newport. **1644** Stradbally. **1645** Dunamaggin. **1646** Castlelyons. **1647** Hospital/Herbertstown. **1648** Castlegar. **1649** Carrig-Riverstown. **1650** St Mark's. **1651** Castletown. **1652** Lámh Dhearg. **1653** Portaferry. **1654** Kevin Lynch's. **1655** Clonkill. **1656** Glenroe. **1657** Kilmoyley. **1658** Keady. **1659** Clarecastle. **1660** Mullinavat.

TIPPERARY GENERAL KNOWLEDGE – page 181

1661 1923. **1662** Offaly. **1663** Kilruane-McDonagh's. **1664** Seamus Butler (his father Tommy was the All-Star winner). **1665** Andy Shorthall. **1666** 1991. **1667** Westmeath. **1668** Eleven. **1669** Tom McGlinchey. **1670** 1999. **1671** Drom-Inch. **1672** Michael 'Babs' Keating. **1673** Michael O'Meara. **1674** Templemore CBS. **1675** Brian Burke. **1676** 1980. **1677** Jodie Grace. **1678** Derry Foley. **1679** Tony Wall. **1680** He became the first son of a Tipperary All-Ireland medal winner to win an All-Ireland on the field of play.

GAA FAMILIES – page 183

1681 Alan, Bernard and Paul Brogan. **1682** Damien and Tommy Freeman. **1683** David and Ger Brady. **1684** Declan and Seamus Prendergast, Ken and Eoin McGrath. **1685** Aaron, Paul, Stephen and Tony Kernan, Armagh. **1686** Mickey and Mark Harte (Tyrone – 2005). **1687** Brian and Simon Whelahan. **1688** Jim and Oisin McConville. **1689** Murt. **1690** Andy and Martin Comerford. **1691** Eamonn and Gary Coleman (Derry – 1993). **1692** Joe and Shane Dooley (Offaly). **1693** Eddie and Willie O'Connor. **1694** Mick O'Dwyer and his sons John (with Kerry) and Karl (with Kildare). **1695** Ollie and Michael Walsh (Kilkenny in 1993). **1696** Paudie and Willie Fitzmaurice (Limerick – 1980). **1697** Maurice and Thomas O'Gorman (Waterford). **1698** John, Joe and Michael Connolly (Galway). **1699** Darragh, Tomás and Marc Ó Sé (Kerry). **1700** Michael O'Grady (Dublin) and PJ O'Grady (Kerry).

OUTSTANDING HURLING AND FOOTBALL GOALS OF THE LAST 10 YEARS – page 185

1701 Owen Mulligan. **1702** Michael Jacob. **1703** Alan Quirke. **1704** Joe Canning. **1705** Clare. **1706** Eamon O'Hara. **1707** Joe Deane. **1708** The replay. **1709** Declan Meehan. **1710** Aidan Kearney. **1711** Ciaran Whelan. **1712** 2006. **1713** Jimmy Coogan. **1714** 2000. **1715** Ronan Clarke. **1716** Eoin Kelly. **1717** Ciaran McManus. **1718** Fergal Healy. **1719** Paul Flynn. **1720** Matthew Clancy.

TYRONE GENERAL KNOWLEDGE – page 188

1721 Conor Gormley. **1722** Ciaran Gourley. **1723** Kevin McNaughton. **1724** Paudge Quinn. **1725** Conor Gormley. **1726** Carrickmore. **1727** Killyclogher. **1728** Coalisland, Trillick and Ardboe. **1729** Danny Ball. **1730** Dugannon Eoghan Rua. **1731** Jody O'Neill. **1732** 2000. **1733** Strabane. **1734** Eugene McKenna. **1735** Declan McCrossan. **1736** Vinny Owens. **1737** Peter Ward. **1738** Eglish. **1739** All-Ireland Vocational Schools Football cup. **1740** Gerry Goodwin.

GENERAL KNOWLEDGE – page 190

1741 An Daingean. **1742** 1997. **1743** 2002. **1744** Vinny Murphy. **1745** Boston. **1746** Damien Fitzhenry. **1747** From a goalkeeper's puckout. **1748** 1994. **1749** Donal Keogan. **1750** Colm Bonnar. **1751** Dublin and Laois in 2003. **1752** Cork and Tipperary in 2007. **1753** Kieran McGeeney (Armagh in 2003). **1754** Colm Callanan. **1755** St Rynagh's. **1756** 2007. **1757** Pat Heffernan. **1758** Thomas Walsh (Wicklow) and Patrick Walsh (Carlow). **1759** 2002. **1760** Karl O'Dwyer (Kerry in 1992, Kildare in 1998 and 2000).

FIRSTS – page 192
1761 1976. **1762** 1928. **1763** 1927. **1764** 1971. **1765** Clare. **1766** 1964. **1767** 1929.
1768 1991. **1769** 1923. **1770** 1974. **1771** London. **1772** 1946. **1773** 1925/26.
1774 1961. **1775** 1944. **1776** The Fitzgibbon Cup. **1777** The Ashbourne Cup (1915).
1778 1913. **1779** 1895. **1780** 1896.

WATERFORD GENERAL KNOWLEDGE – page 194
1781 Ken McGrath, Dan Shanahan, Stephen Molumphy and Michael Walsh. **1782** The Nire, Stradbally, Kilrossanty and Ballinacourty. **1783** Nicky Cashin, Michael Ryan and Seamie Hannon. **1784** 1994, 1995. **1785** Michael 'Brick' Walsh. **1786** Blackrock. **1787** Rathgormack. **1788** Liam Fennelly. **1789** Bull. **1790** Ballygunner. **1791** John Galvin. **1792** Derek McGrath. **1793** John Cummins. **1794** Jim Fives. **1795** John Hennessy. **1796** Danny Purcell. **1797** Thomas O'Gorman. **1798** Mick Fennelly. **1799** Frankie Walsh (1960). **1800** Jim Greene.

NOTEWORTHY ACHIEVEMENTS AND RECORDS IN HURLING AND FOOTBALL – page 196
1801 18. **1802** 11. **1803** Paul McGrane. **1804** Ray Cummins. **1805** Pat, Ger and John Henderson (Kilkenny). **1806** Frank Cummins. **1807** Nicky Rackard. **1808** True. **1809** Eddie Keher (Kilkenny). **1810** John Mullane (Waterford). **1811** James McCartan Snr (Down), Jimmy Keaveney (Dublin) and Jack O'Shea (Kerry) (O'Shea won consecutive awards twice). **1812** Mick, John Michael and John Donnellan. **1813** Michael Kavanagh. **1814** Peter McDermott. **1815** Jimmy Barry-Murphy. **1816** Three. **1817** Limerick. **1818** 'Danno' O'Keeffe. **1819** Jackie Power, Ger Power and Stephen McNamara. **1820** Seamus Looney (Cork).

HURLING ALL-STARS – page 199
1821 Brian Murray (Limerick). **1822** Michael Kavanagh and Jackie Tyrrell. **1823** Brendan Cummins (Tipperary). **1824** Ollie Moran and Andrew O'Shaughnessy. **1825** Declan Fanning. **1826** Ollie Canning. **1827** Davy Fitzgerald and Jamesie O'Connor. **1828** 2002 and 2005. **1829** John Gardiner (Cork). **1830** 2002. **1831** Brian Corcoran. **1832** Pat McLoughney and Ken Hogan. **1833** Brian Whelahan (Offaly) and Brian Corcoran (Cork). **1834** Henry Shefflin. **1835** Kilkenny. **1836** Pat Harhgan (Limerick) and Eddie Keher (Kilkenny). **1837** Aidan and Bobby Ryan. **1838** Denis Coughlan. **1839** Five. **1840** Tony Browne (Waterford).

WESTMEATH GENERAL KNOWLEDGE – page 201
1841 Gary Connaughton and Dessie Dolan. **1842** Three. **1843** PJ Qualter. **1844** Derry. **1845** Brendan Murtagh. **1846** Carmelite College, Moate (they won three titles). **1847** John Cooney. **1848** Brendan Lowry. **1849** 'Jobber' McGrath. **1850** Darren

McCormack. **1851** Damien Healy. **1852** Maryland. **1853** David Mitchell. **1854** 1932.
1855 Tyrrellspass, Athlone and The Downs. **1856** The ball was dropped from an
aeroplane to start the first game. **1857** Martin Flanagan. **1858** 1982. **1859** John Shaw.
1860 Six.

HURLING GENERAL KNOWLEDGE – page 204
1861 Terence 'Sambo' McNaughton and Dominic 'Woody' McKinley. **1862** Liam
Mellows. **1863** Galway and Cork. **1864** Eddie Keher (Kilkenny). **1865** Michael Conneely.
1866 Nicky Rackard (Wexford). **1867** Chunky. **1868** 1996. **1869** Conor Hayes (Galway).
1870 Eddie Keher, Pat Henderson, Ollie Walsh and Brian Cody. **1871** Mikey Maher
(Tipperary), Christy Ring (Cork) and Conor Hayes (Galway). **1872** Toronto Skydome.
1873 Seven. **1874** Kilkenny and Dublin. **1875** Broderick was playing with
St Raphael's, Loughrea while Deane lined out with Midleton CBS. **1876** Tipperary.
1877 Paddy McMahon (Limerick), Tony Doran and Nicky Rackard (Wexford).
1878 Kevin Fennelly (Kilkenny – 1978 and 1987). **1879** Mark Corrigan. **1880** Martin
Kennedy (Tipperary) – The 1932 National hurling league final was staged in Portumna
between Galway and Tipperary and the local parish priest decided that neither side
should leave the field empty handed so he acquired two cups, which he presented to
the respective captains.

CLUB HURLING AND FOOTBALL – page 206
1881 Mickey Whelan. **1882** 1992 (Kiltormer and Cashel King Cormacs had drawn their
replayed match on March 8th so the semi-final was still outstanding). **1883** East
Kerry. **1884** Newtownshandrum. **1885** Andy Smith (Portumna in 2007 and UCD in
2004). **1886** Ephie Fitzgerald. **1887** Sixmilebridge, Wolfe Tones and St Joseph's Doora-
Barefield. **1888** Bellaghy, Lavey and Ballinderry. **1889** Joe Rabbitte. **1890** Thomond
College Limerick. **1891** Castlegar (1980). **1892** 2000. **1893** St Joseph's Doora-Barefield
(Clare). **1894** Niall Geary. **1895** Pad Joe Whelahan (Birr) and Pat Nally (Athenry).
1896 Tony Doran (Buffers Alley). **1897** Donal Murtagh (Crossmaglen Rangers), Billy
Morgan (Nemo Rangers) and Mickey Whelan (St Vincent's). **1898** Manchester.
1899 Loughmore-Castleleiney (Tipperary). **1900** Gerry Keane, Paul Hardiman and Pat
Higgins (Athenry).

WEXFORD GENERAL KNOWLEDGE – page 208
1901 True. **1902** Skippy. **1903** 1999. **1904** Aidan O'Brien. **1905** Nicky Rackard and
Tony Doran. **1906** Redmond Barry. **1907** Malachy Travers. **1908** 1956. **1909** Barry
Lambert. **1910** 1992. **1911** Colm Doran and Martin Quigley. **1912** Rod Guiney.
1913 St Peter's, Wexford. **1914** Diarmuid and Ciaran Lyng. **1915** Oulart-the-Ballagh.
1916 Colm and Tony Doran, Martin and John Quigley. **1917** Christy Kehoe. **1918** Jim
Byrne, Gus Kennedy, Tom Doyle, Paddy Mackey, Tom Murphy, Martin Howlett and
Aidan Doyle. **1919** Adamstown and Shelmaliers. **1920** Sean O'Kennedy and
Paddy Mackey.

HURLERS TURNED REFEREES – page 210

1921 True. **1922** 1980. **1923** Clare. **1924** Con Murphy. **1925** Tommy Daly. **1926** Jimmy Langton (Kilkenny). **1927** Donie Nealon. **1928** Cork. **1929** Jimmy Smyth. **1930** 1923. **1931** Snitchie. **1932** Inky. **1933** Tipperary. **1934** Clare. **1935** Kilkenny. **1936** Tipperary. **1937** Paddy Buggy (Kilkenny). **1938** Jimmy Grey. **1939** Michael Haverty (he played with Loughrea in the 2007 All-Ireland club final). **1940** Vin Baston.

CONTROVERSIAL MANAGERIAL RESIGNATIONS AND UPHEAVALS – page 213

1941 Justin McCarthy (Waterford). **1942** Mickey Moran (Mayo). **1943** Clare. **1944** Bertie Óg Murphy. **1945** Brian McDonald. **1946** Pad Joe Whelahan. **1947** Mickey Whelan. **1948** Dom Corrigan. **1949** Nickey Brennan. **1950** 2001. **1951** Paul Earley. **1952** James Kearns. **1953** Damien Fox (Laois). **1954** Eamonn Barry. **1955** Mattie Murphy. **1956** Humphrey Kelleher. **1957** Ger Halligan. **1958** Mick Condon. **1959** Kevin Fennelly (Kilkenny in 1998) and John Allen (Cork in 2006). **1960** Johnny Pilkington.

WICKLOW GENERAL KNOWLEDGE – page 216

1961 Tommy Gill. **1962** Two. **1963** Aughrim. **1964** Two. **1965** An Tóchar. **1966** Clann na nGael (Roscommon). **1967** Hugh Kenny. **1968** Blessington. **1969** Na Fianna. **1970** Hugh Byrne. **1971** True. **1972** Kevin O'Brien and Pat O'Byrne. **1973** Tinahely. **1974** John Henderson. **1975** Gerry O'Reilly. **1976** Dave Foran. **1977** Eamonn Moules and Jimmy Hatton. **1978** Niall Rennick. **1979** Jimmy Hatton. **1980** Kilmacud Crokes.

GENERAL KNOWLEDGE – page 218

1981 Declan and Kenneth O'Keeffe with Kerry in 1996. **1982** Kilkenny. **1983** Napier University Edinburgh Scotland. **1984** Michael O'Grady. **1985** Seán Óg Ó hAilpín (Cork) and Conal Keaney (Dublin). **1986** Andy Smith (Galway) and Leo Smith (Westmeath). **1987** 1979 Ulster Football Final, Donegal v Monaghan. **1988** Alan and Mark Kerins (Galway), Seán Óg and Setanta Ó hAilpín (Cork). **1989** Michael Foley (Leitrim) and Alan Foley (New York). **1990** Noel Keane (Clonoulty/Rossmore – Tipperary – 1997 and Blackrock – Cork – 1999). **1991** Brian Murphy (Cork hurlers – 1992, Kildare footballers – 1998). **1992** Andy Comerford (London in 1995 and Kilkenny in 2002). **1993** Joe McGrath (Sarsfields and Galway – 1993). **1994** Tommy Walsh (Kerry). **1995** Noel Lane (Galway). **1996** Rory Gallagher (St Brigid's Dublin in 2003), Ronan Gallagher (St Gall's Antrim in 2007). **1997** 1984. **1998** Midleton (football 1890, hurling 1984). **1999** Joe McDonagh and his son Eoin, who captained Galway in the 1997 All-Ireland minor final against Clare. **2000** Michael Braniff (Down v Antrim, 2001 Ulster hurling semi-final).